Children between the Wars

American Childhood, 1920–1940

Twayne's History of American Childhood Series

Series Editors
Joseph M. Hawes, Memphis State University
N. Ray Hiner, University of Kansas

Children between the Wars

American Childhood, 1920–1940

Joseph M. Hawes

Twayne Publishers
An Imprint of Simon & Schuster Macmillan
New York

Prentice Hall International
London • Mexico City • New Delhi • Singapore • Sydney • Toronto

Twayne Publishers
An Imprint of Simon & Schuster Macmillan
1633 Broadway
New York, NY 10019

Library of Congress Cataloging-in-Publication Data
Hawes, Joseph M.
    Children between the wars : American childhood, 1920–1940 / Joseph
M. Hawes
        p.   cm. — (Twayne's history of American childhood series)
    Includes bibliographical references and index.
    ISBN 0-8057-4114-3
    1. Children—United States—Social conditions. 2. Children—
United States—History—20th century. 3. United States—Social
conditions—1918–1932. 4. United States—Social
conditions—1933–1945.   I. Title.   II. Series.
HQ792.U5H3   1997
305.23'0973—dc21   97-36626
                                                                                        CIP

This paper meets the requirements of ANSI/NISO Z3948–1992 Permanence of Paper.

10 9 8 7 6 5 4 3 2 1

Printed in the United States of America

This book is dedicated to Gail, Lyda,
Kristen, Greg, Erin, and John.

Contents

Series Editor's Note

The history of children is coming of age. What began in the 1960's as a spontaneous response by some historians to the highly visible and sometimes unsettling effects of the baby boom, has emerged as a vigorous and broad-based inquiry into the lives of American children in all generations. As this series on American Childhood attests, this new field is robust and includes the work of scholars from a variety of disciplines.

Our goal for this series is to introduce this rich and expanding field to academics and to general readers interested in children and their place in history. All of the books provide important insight into the changing shape and character of children's lives in America. Finally, this series demonstrates very clearly that children are and always have been influential historical actors in their own right. Children play an essential role in the American story that this series is designed to illuminate.

Children Between the Wars examines the interaction among experts, society, and children during the two decades between 1920 and 1940. Experts dominated the discussion on one side, while parents listened anxiously to the experts and tried to put their advice into practice. Meanwhile, children and youth, who were attending age-graded schools in greater numbers and for longer periods, turned increasingly to their peers for advice, and young people, especially, created norms of sociability that often shocked their elders. By 1920 Progressivism had lost most of its energy, but political and social reformers continued to support legislation to reduce infant mortality and restrict child labor even though their efforts were only marginally successful during the 1920's.

The Great Depression had a tremendous impact on children and youth. Some families were so poor that they could not afford basic health care, and some children suffered from poor diets that could lead to malnutrition and even death. While New Deal programs provided important assistance to many children and their families, the harmful effects of the depression on child health care can be seen in the poor physical condition of many World War II inductees. By the end of the 1930's the experts and the government, worried about the rise of fascism in Europe, focused their attention on promoting democracy among young people, who had begun to learn about it for themselves in their expanding peer groups.

N. Ray Hiner
University of Kansas

Illustrations

Preface

In a way, this book continues the story of the relationship between the state and youthful offenders that I began in my first book, *Children in Urban Society: Juvenile Delinquency in the Nineteenth Century*.[1] In the 25 years between these two books, my interest in children and childhood has broadened considerably, so that this work is an expansion of my own concerns as well as a continuation of an earlier work. It is also a volume in a series that I coedit with N. Ray Hiner and as such is limited in terms of chronology and scope. It also represents a continuation of another sort. As I finished *Children in Urban Society,* I became interested in the discipline of child psychology and its role in the shaping of modern society. Other tasks and works took me away from that interest, and now this work has brought me back. The delay was fortunate because in the interim, an army of scholars have been digging away at such topics as the history of child development research, child guidance clinics, the Federal Children's Bureau, and the National Youth Administration, to name just a few of the many helpful works.[2] My purpose in this brief synthesis is to pull together an overview of the main developments in the United States affecting American children and also the evolving social construction of childhood in the crucial years between World Wars I and II. I think this period marked the emergence of modern America, an America unlike anything in earlier decades. This transformation meant that school attendance would be compulsory for all children, usually through age 16, so that school attendance would be a common experience for most Americans for the remainder of the twentieth century. This was the era in which science enjoyed unprecedented social prestige and the time when a special science of "normal" children emerged and began to guide the parenting styles of most Americans. This was a period when parenting became both an object of study and a discipline to be taught. Children and youths, in spite of the greater regimentation of their lives, gained greater control over some portions of their lives through the use of peer groups. In order to understand American society after World War II, it is necessary to look very closely at the interwar years—the subject of this work.

Acknowledgments

Portions of the research for this book were supported by a Bordin-Gillete Researcher Travel Fellowship from the Bentley Historical Library of the University of Michigan. Additional support came from the University of Memphis and a Professional Development Assignment. I am grateful for the support and assistance of David Van Tassel of Case Western Reserve, who provided guidance, access to the history faculty at Case Western Reserve, and hospitality. I am similarly grateful to Jane Schnell of Washington, D.C., who provided hospitality while I worked at the National Library of Medicine, the Library of Congress, and the National Archives. The staffs of all the repositories already noted as well as the History of Psychology Archives at the University of Akron and the Western Reserve Historical Society Library and Archives were unfailingly helpful and courteous and did a great deal to smooth the way for this project.

I appreciate as well the helpful suggestions made by members of the Child and Family Colloquium of the Psychology Department of the University of Memphis, the History Department at Case Western Reserve, and the history seminar series at the University of Memphis, who responded to draft portions of this work. I owe a special debt to Hamilton Cravens of Iowa State University for his continued support, encouragement, and groundbreaking work in the field. Similarly, I must acknowledge that this work could not have been possible without the support and encouragement of my coeditor and collaborator, N. Ray Hiner. Some portions of this manuscript have also been presented to the Mid America History Conference and the Great Lakes History Conference. I appreciate the helpful comments received at those meetings. The errors of fact and judgment that remain are mine alone.

1

Young Americans, 1920–1940: An Overview

The purpose of this book is to identify national trends in the history of children and youth in the United States between World War I and World War II. Separate chapters are devoted to the rise of peer groups (which coincided with the growth of graded schools and compulsory school attendance laws); the expansion of education during the 1920s (there were more children in more schools for longer periods of time); the expansion of the American educational establishment; the rise of the United States Children's Bureau (although created in 1912, this federal agency came into its own in the 1920s and played a major role in social legislation in the 1930s); the rise of the experts (the combination of the creation of child psychology as an academic specialty and the expansion of child guidance clinics and school psychology created a national body of professional expertise about American children, and experts in these fields promoted standardized, "scientifically based" child-rearing advice); the growth of social agencies and their impact on children and families; and finally the importance of the Great Depression and the New Deal for children and young people (children experienced hardship but also found strength in the depression, whereas the effects of the New Deal, including social programs such as the National Youth Administration and legislation such as the Social Security Act and the Fair Labor Standards Act, were mostly positive).

Probably the most important development concerning children of this period was the increased prominence of "experts" in society and their role in shaping public attitudes and policies toward children and youth. These new experts came from a variety of disciplines, but psychology, psychiatry, and social work dominated, along with the family studies aspects of home economics. Experts sought relationships with the schools and in some cases included teachers as professional colleagues in their schemes to fix or improve the problems of children and youth. These professionals believed that their goal and social role was to use their expertise to remedy social ills and thus shape the future of society. As children and youth were more pliable, relatively easy to access, and the future leaders of society, they were the obvious means whereby the new professionals might put their expertise and theories to work.

The two decades between the world wars were a time of great expansion of the social policy sciences in the academy and of the child- and family-oriented specialties among the helping professions. These specialties grew because of lingering progressivism among intellectuals and academics and because of public fascination with science and expertise. The public thought that these social technicians were capable of fixing social ills because they were systematic, rational, and willing to work with children. Having developed a body of arcane knowledge, the new professionals were eager to put their expertise to work on the myriad ills of society. The professionals' prestige and numbers did not diminish during the Great Depression because they had only just begun to apply their knowledge to society. By 1930 they had convinced most thoughtful Americans that a great many children and youth were in trouble and in need of professional help. The nation was more than ready to let the experts—the people who told them the young folks had problems—try to solve those problems during the crisis of the 1930s.[1]

The corridors of power among the social scientists were bastions of white male privilege, but the exclusion of women had one ironic and positive effect. Because working with children brought relatively low prestige, many of the outstanding women who received doctorates in psychology were channeled into children's work. Thus child science benefited from the work of people such as Leta S. Hollingworth, Jean W. Macfarlane, Nancy Bailey, Helen Thompson Woolley, Mary Cover Jones, Lois Meek Stolz, Lois B. Murphy, Beth Wellman, and Florence Goodenough, to name only a few of the many women who made important contributions to the field of child science in the twenties and thirties.[2]

A second, equally important development was the rise of peer groups among young people. Fraternities and sororities and their role in both socializing young people into the larger society and providing the protection young people needed as they experimented with various means of personal expression were the most visible forms of peer groups, but the schools and the streets also fostered peer groups that functioned in similar ways. As American society became more urban and thus more fragmented, young people developed their own communities to replace the lost worlds of small-town America.[3]

As for the children and youth themselves, they found an America still willing to let young children work in dangerous factories and cotton mills. The coalition of reformers who had pushed for the passage of the Keating Owen Act of 1916 found that they could not muster the political strength necessary to win ratification for an amendment to the Constitution to ban child labor at the federal level once the Supreme Court had thrown out the act in the case of *Hammer v. Dagenhart*. Attention to state laws and campaigns in the media would be the main efforts of child labor reformers until the Great Depression changed the political climate enough that a federal law (the Fair Labor Standards Act) could pass constitutional muster with a chastened Supreme Court.

At the same time, school attendance increased and child labor declined because more children and youth were in school and were staying in school longer. The new compulsory school attendance laws proved more effective in keeping young people out of dangerous occupations than did the child labor laws themselves. And new technology enabled industry to reduce or eliminate the need for large numbers of unskilled laborers. In the twentieth century, public schools became universal, and the nation saw virtually all its children attend school at least for some part of the elementary curriculum. High school attendance was up, too. As a result of the expansion of education, most young Americans now had the common experience of school attendance. Young people began to think of themselves in terms of their ages and grades, and young America became much more rigidly stratified. As a defense against this intrusion of adult authority into the lives of young people, children and youth created their own world after school. In large cities, they did this on the streets, and on college campuses, fraternities and sororities organized peer groups to give young people both greater personal freedom and greater social security.[4]

In the cities, the streets helped to socialize children into the realities of urban American life. No child who grew up on the streets could miss the hierarchical way society was organized or the essential democracy of street life. The children played games and graduated from one level of sophistication to another depending on age and ability. Parents and other adults supervised the activities of young people from a distance and allowed them to settle their own disputes according to their own rules. Some children worked after school, selling newspapers or candy or shining shoes. They recognized the turf of individual newsies, organized themselves democratically, and on at least one occasion successfully struck the major New York daily newspapers. Suburban delivery and worsening economic times gradually drove most of the newsies off the streets, but the rich social life of the streets and urban neighborhoods continued. By means of peer groups, young people gained greater freedom and control over their own lives.

Some urban agencies, notably churches and child-helping agencies, tried to establish adult-run quasi peer groups for young people: Boy Scouts, Girl Scouts, Girl Guides, Girls' and Boys' Clubs, Cub Scouts, Brownies, and various church-sponsored youth groups. These adult-sponsored organizations brought young people together to learn a variety of values not taught or advocated in the schools or in homes of immigrant and working-class families. These adult-sponsored groups indicated that adults understood the appeal of peer groups while also indicating the wish of young people to control their own lives. At times, young people could use these adult-sponsored groups for their own purposes, relying on the adult leaders to furnish a shield from excessive scrutiny from the adult world as young people explored their own issues.

The differences between adult-sponsored peer groups and those developed by the children and youth themselves are of major significance. Young people needed some freedom from adult supervision to develop their own standards and values; adults were trying to prevent young people from doing just that. Adults had their own ideas about what children and youth should think and do, and the notion that young people could arrive at their own codes of behavior seemed at best troubling and at worst threatening to the very foundations of society. As a result, young people learned to protect their freedom by using the peer groups as a shield, a kind of front. Fraternities and sororities participated in a host of adult-sponsored, wholesome activities as a kind of front to protect the organizations from closer scrutiny when they held dances and parties and otherwise indulged in youthful exuberance. Similarly, newsboys engaged in the street trades in large American cities developed their own rules for the allocation of turf, settled disputes democratically, and protected each other when the police or reformers threatened the boys' trade or territory.

There was a continuous struggle between children and adults over the values and behaviors of the young people themselves. Ironically both attempted to use peer groups for their own purposes. Adults expected to lead and influence the direction of the groups they sponsored, and young people used their own groups as a shield between themselves and adult authority. Using the power of the law and civic authority, adults gradually gained some control over some urban streets, though urban residential streets continued to belong in large part to the young people who lived there. But older children and youth maintained their prerogatives despite adult efforts to influence their peer groups. Fraternities and sororities became adept at presenting one face to the adults nominally in charge of their activities and quite another to members and potential recruits.

Many national trends of the twenties touched on or included young people. The rise of mass culture included many aspects aimed directly at children and youth. Movies, in particular, appealed to children who had money to spend and an eye for vicarious excitement and adventure. Young people flocked to the movies that had exciting themes and thrills, whereas more serious drama and educational fare quickly disappeared when it was unable to attract consistent support. In effect, the children themselves determined what played at the local cinema. They patronized penny arcades and candy stores and other places set up to provide the goods desired by young people who now had money of their own to spend. Thus the rise of the consumer culture included youth as well as the new urban middle classes, and young people helped to determine what was offered.[5]

Automobiles, too, had a major impact on youth. Families were more mobile. Visits to relatives and vacation trips to resorts, seashores, and mountains became more common. For young people, however, the automobile provided unprecedented freedom of movement and privacy. By themselves, automobiles did not transform youthful behavior, but in concert with the rise of peer groups and the increasing independence of youth, automobiles enabled young people to range far and wide and to enjoy personal privacy in the process. Did this mean increased sexual activity? Yes and no. There was more experimentation. "Petting" became the standard form of sexual experimentation, but codes developed by peer groups and well understood by most young people set limits short of actual intercourse.

Family life underwent major transformations in the twenties, or perhaps society as a whole became more aware of some long-term demographic and dynamic trends. Middle-class families had been getting smaller since the time of the American Revolution, but society did not apparently become aware of this trend until the 1920s. (Theodore Roosevelt and some of the demographers of his day had noticed and talked about it, but the larger society paid little attention at that time.) Some experts saw the shrinking size of the family as a problem, but most came to see it as the new American norm. A smaller middle-class family could be more democratic (the obverse image the experts cited was the urban immigrant family, which they saw as authoritarian and backward). Family meetings would replace patriarchal decision making, and parents and children would interact on the basis of mutual respect. Husbands and wives would be companions, friends, and partners facing life's challenges. These were the images and the realities within which these families appeared to fit.

Children were more independent because there was little need to apply strict discipline to them. They were more independent because many of them had money of their own, earned from work after school or from a family allowance. Immigrant families, perhaps expecting to continue old-country ways, found that their working children used the money they earned to attain a measure of independence. They did this by buying, dressing, acting, and speaking "American." Young women in particular rejected the sacrificial and moral role of their mothers and began to explore the possibilities life offered. Many young women talked of careers and wondered how it might be possible to combine a family and a career. They also rejected the notion that women were somehow asexual beings and above the carnal nature of human lust.

This newfound freedom, this revolt against the authority of the older generation, had many sources. Young people had money of their own; they had seen the values of their parents rejected in the trenches of northern France; they sensed the national mood of indulgence and a retreat from serious things such as progressive reform; they saw the many hypocrisies of a society being transformed from rural and agrarian to urban and industrial; they learned how to have fun by watching other young people in the movies; and they learned from each other through peer groups at school and on the streets how to avoid the heavy hand of adult authority. These changes presented parents with a number of dilemmas. How could they keep the kids under control? How could they preserve a daughter's reputation or a son's chances at success? How could they discharge parental duties and inculcate the proper values when their children spent less and less time at home around the hearth, the piano, or the dinner table?

Parents hoped the schools would do some of this work, and organizations such as the PTA encouraged the schools to give more attention to morals and values so that young people's and society's futures would not be jeopardized by youthful rebellion. Parents wanted to censor movies and restrict children's access to them; they wanted to control listening to the radio and limit young people's time away from home in various forms of unsupervised play. So a constant struggle between parents and children characterized home life in the twenties. Home was boring and dull. Streets full of children and movies and amusements were exciting and within the means and reach of most urban kids. As hard as parents tried to maintain a tight leash, they were never able to do much more than limit the new influences on their children.[6]

So fathers and mothers saw their influence decline, their parental authority undermined and their values and attitudes questioned, but they also saw their children rebelling in only limited ways. Few middle-class children left home permanently while in their early teens or younger; few of them openly challenged parental authority or indicated that they had totally rejected family life; and most maintained strong family ties even after they had moved away from home. What the young people were doing without fully realizing it was changing the dynamics of family life—the way families actually worked. Children needed more freedom to explore the myriad possibilities urban life afforded; they needed more freedom to learn who they were and how they would relate to this varied and confusing world; they also needed a safe haven, a place for retreat when they needed to regroup. Girls seemed to know instinctively that the old patterns their mothers lived by were not adequate for the modern world young people faced; they needed a different kind of help to succeed in life. The young men of the 1920s were less interested in the image of refinement and virtue women of the nineteenth century cultivated; young men wanted a companion, someone with whom to share the excitement and the possibilities of life. A corseted and bustled figurine would scarcely do. And young women needed the same freedom to explore the same set of possibilities for themselves. Perhaps they would not marry. Never before had this seemed so possible. Perhaps they would develop a career and then later choose to marry and have a family. This too seemed more likely than ever before.[7]

A survivor of the Progressive Era, the Federal Children's Bureau blossomed between the wars. The bureau mounted a number of initiatives, such as juvenile delinquency prevention projects; surveys of mentally defective children; advocacy of special education, mental hygiene, and child guidance clinics; and a series of advice manuals and related publications. The bureau also played an important role in the crusade against child labor and in the drafting of the Social Security Act. The federal government, in response to the novelty of voting by women, passed the Sheppard-Towner Act, which granted federal money to states for preventative prenatal programs designed to lower infant mortality rates. An enormous success, the Sheppard-Towner Act nevertheless fell victim to the interests of regular M.D.'s and was not extended after 1928.[8]

Meanwhile, parents turned to experts to see how to address the problem of rebellious youth. In both the 1920s and the 1930s, many Americans believed that youth was in crisis (although for different reasons). In part the crisis was created by the professionals with substantial aid from the Laura Spelman Rockefeller Memorial and Lawrence K. Frank. There was a virtual explosion of professional child helping in the 1920s: the establishment of child guidance clinics and psychological clinics such as the Judge Baker Clinic, associated with the Juvenile Court in Boston, or the Juvenile Psychopathological Clinic in Chicago, the rise of developmental and child psychology as specialties, and the growth of family studies, especially in sociology and home economics. These specialties and subdisciplines had existed before World War I, but although the reaction to the war seemed to kill off progressivism, it paradoxically increased public support of the social sciences, especially those pertaining to children and families.

Yes, there was a problem, the experts said. In fact, there were many problems. Some children, especially many of those engaged in the street trades, came from immigrant families who did not understand American values and practices. A solution to this problem would be for social workers and their allies (possibly teachers and juvenile court judges) to find ways to intervene in these families and teach them how to live life properly in a modern American city. Children were a precious resource, so they needed to be helped or saved.

After the war, American society took a number of steps to approach this problem in a more holistic fashion. First, immigration was restricted, reducing the number of migrants from central and southern Europe to a trickle. Then, because the federal child labor law had been declared unconstitutional, reformers and professionals shifted their strategy to compulsory school attendance laws as a way to get the kids off the streets and out of the factories. They also tried to control the after-school behavior of urban children, limiting hours of movie houses and other forms of amusement. At the same time, they expanded the role of the juvenile court and used it as net, casting among the many children on the streets and bringing in those most in need of help. The idea was that the court would serve as a referral agency to all the professional help available in the city. In some cities, such as Chicago and Boston, clinics were attached directly to the court.

The underlying assumption was that misbehaving kids had something wrong with them that could be fixed—by the experts who made it their business to study the pathology of youth. At the time, no one seems to have understood that the psychologists and other experts had a vested interest in finding psychopathology in troubled youth and thus exhibited little difficulty in doing so. No one, that is, except perhaps William A. Healy, a psychiatrist attached to the Chicago clinic and later to the Judge Baker Clinic. Healy could find little or no psychopathology among the young people he studied, pointing instead to social factors.[9]

That the new social science professionals found an abundance of social problems is hardly surprising. Earlier interpretations have suggested that such findings stemmed from a desire to make various aspects of the social sciences into policy sciences. This in turn would transform the social scientists themselves into policy makers, advice givers, and expert technocrats who could use their knowledge and power to transform society. Their goals in this view, then, included a desire to wield more influence and to control the unruly elements of society.

This line of analysis raises some difficult questions for the historian. Were social scientists and their professional allies primarily motivated by a desire to control the lower orders of society or, as this book suggests, children, the future members of society? Was their principal motivation essentially a lust for power? The answer depends on how the question is phrased. Did they wish to become social and moral police? Probably not. Did they wish to monitor the lives of all Americans? They undoubtedly realized the impossibility of such a task. Did they wish to be a part of a new police state organized around the ideology of modernism and technocracy? The Nazi example forces us to examine this question more closely. That there were elements of racism (especially in the guise of eugenics) among American social scientists was certainly true, although some, notably Franz Boas and Else Clews Parson, worked to reduce racism and ethnocentrism from national policy. Were they willing to "sell" their expertise to government and private agencies in the name of science and progress? Yes, most definitely, as the experience of various New Deal agencies or of the agencies blessed by grants from the Laura Spelman Rockefeller Memorial indicate. But were these efforts a grab for power? Were they in the service of a compelling, all-encompassing ideology? No, the German and American experiences do not really compare; there was no seizure of power by a minority political group as had been the case in Germany. Would the social scientists have signed on in a Nazi America? This of course is an unanswerable question, but the thrust of their efforts was to advocate two values antithetical to totalitarianism: a democratic family and a process of self-actualization that promoted social individualism. The power the social scientists sought was not primarily political. If anything, it was intellectual. They wished to be respected and taken seriously; they hoped that their expertise might be ameliorative rather than oppressive. They honestly believed that their great enterprise would result in better social and individual life. Thus we can conclude that they were not primarily motivated by desires for social control per se.[10]

The impact of the efforts of social scientists was of a different order, however. Motivations alone do not determine the social functions of any group or agency. The best of intentions can lead to the most terrible of consequences. Probably the most damaging effect of the experts was their seemingly innocent view that certain forms of behavior were normal and that any variation from them was therefore deviant. The experts' focus was narrow and shaped by their own ethnocentrism. They were virtually all white males, and they believed their purpose was to encourage the freedom and success of young white males. They worried, for example, about the "boy problem," and could not understand that there might be a corresponding "girl problem." In their view, girls were a problem only if they were sexually active. The experts defined middle-class Anglo-Saxon families as normal and regarded the families of Jewish and Italian immigrants as pathological, even though immigrant family structure helped millions of people adjust to, and cope with, American industrial society. In effect, the social scientists' great failing was eagerness. They wanted to be taken seriously by society, so when they had learned a little about individual psychological development and family dynamics, they began to "sell" what they had learned to social agencies, governments, schools, and the public.

The new expertise was enormously helpful to young white males even as it was conveyed by outstanding women in the helping professions. Young men's search for identity and a life's calling received full social support and generous government funding during the New Deal. The effect of the new social sciences on young white women was more mixed. Their rebellion against Victorian conventions in the 1920s was justified by the new social science expertise—particularly by the work of the women who had entered the social science professions. Yet the gains young white women were beginning to make evaporated in the Great Depression. Very few women social scientists were able to secure stable, "regular" professional positions in the twenties and thirties. Consequently their voices were rarely heard in the cacophony of demands that pressed on New Dealers in the early months and years of Roosevelt's first term. New Deal programs for youth were almost all for young males and posited a white middle-class family as the social institution being aided or preserved.[11]

Other young Americans fared less well. The amount of space they received in the universe of social science discourse was limited. Native Americans did have some advocates, such as the famous "red progressives," and the Merriam Report of 1928 called attention to the sad state of most Indians, but there was little, if any, thought given to promoting the psychological development of Native American youth of either sex. John Collier's efforts led to the passage of the Wheeler-Howard Act in 1934, which restored tribal government and generated some awareness of the unique needs of Native American children and youth, but Collier's focus was political rather than educational. A similar case could be made regarding African-American youth and families. Although the work of E. Franklin Frazier focused on African-American families, it did so in a context that saw those families as pathological, having been permanently damaged by the experience of slavery. In effect, Frazier's work reinforced the normative views of the mainstream family and child experts.[12]

Were the patterns for African-American children similar to those for other children? The answer to this question must be mixed. The great migration north was already under way, though the tide would swell after World War II. African-American children in the rural South saw few changes in their lives before the Civil Rights movement. Their schools were woefully inadequate by any measure: the buildings were in poor repair; books, laboratory equipment, and other teaching aids were out of date or nonexistent; and teachers' salaries were much lower than those of their white counterparts. The situation for African-Americans in northern cities was rarely ideal, although public services tended to be better funded. The schools were adequately supplied and kept, but they were often racially segregated. Even under the best of circumstances, however, African-American families' incomes were only a fraction of the average white family's income, and given these stresses, it was much more difficult for African-American youth to remain in school when by working they could contribute to the family income. African-American wives and mothers were more likely to work than native-born or immigrant wives and hoped, through their labor, to enable their children to gain greater access to education. Yet few African-American families could find stable employment at a level that would enable children to remain in school through high school, let alone college. Pervasive prejudice and racism, even when not codified by law as in the segregated South, confined African-Americans to the lowest rungs of society and denied them access to the emerging middle-class society of urban America.

The lives of American children and young people changed dramatically during the 1920s and the 1930s. Children's lives changed because American society was transformed. Rural small-town America had become modern urban America. In 1920, for the first time, more Americans lived in cities than in small towns or the rural countryside. Living in the city had an enormous effect on family life, on social patterns, and on the process of growing up and leaving home. No longer would most Americans grow into maturity in the same face-to-face community their parents had. Now most Americans would undergo the metropolitan experience that a few urban pioneers had undergone since the beginning of the nineteenth century. Thus a new national and urban American pattern emerged in the interwar years. It was a pattern shaped by experts, transmitted by national media, and aimed primarily at the nation's young people. The dream of remaking America that had energized the Progressive Era remained, but now the means had changed. Legislation and exhortation would give way to social expertise and an expanded, centrally important public-school system, a system that would socialize all its pupils into the modern metropolitan culture of postwar America. Young people, very much aware of the agenda that society and the experts had for them, joined peer groups in order to create a protective shield, behind which they could experiment and develop their own rules of life.

American life could be seen as a three-way struggle between modernizers, traditionalists, and young people. The modernizers wished to create a modern, hierarchical, and democratic state organized around the principles of science, modernity, and expertise. The traditionalists wanted a return to main street and the virtues of small-town America. Young people wished to enjoy the freedom and excitement of modern America—jazz, gin, and sex—but they wished to develop and enforce their own rules without parental or societal influence. The Great Depression altered the agendas of all three but did not destroy their basic design. For many young people, the depression meant the end of, or the postponement of, their dreams, but their determination to be free from earlier conventions seldom wavered. Modernists quickly enlisted in the cause of the New Deal and found, through government programs, new means for pushing their agendas. Traditionalists were heartened by the collapse of big business and hoped that metropolitan America would follow suit. Small towns may have enjoyed a brief reflowering, but the trend toward urbanization and a national culture continued. Movies, radio, and literature continued to expand and shape a national vision of what it meant to be an American.

Had a new version of American childhood been constructed in the years between the world wars? Yes, because the existence of a national youth culture and a national youth market was new, but much of the old America remained. Families, if smaller on the whole, were still the primary socializing agents of the young. The expansion of public education had altered the lives of young people in ways that remained unchanged throughout the century. School attendance was now a common experience for virtually all Americans. Thus young people found themselves in a new relation to government and the state. As the state had entered directly into their lives, children and youth related to public society more as individuals than as family members. In the same way, they related to sellers of candy and movie tickets. Families were thus less able to protect young people from the designs of government or the marketplace. Children had more freedom, then, but less protection.

However, children were probably healthier in 1940 than they had been in 1920. Many draftees during World War II were rejected because of poor health, but the situation was not nearly so drastic as it had been during the first war. The Sheppard-Towner Act had reduced infant mortality on a national scale. In addition, improved access to health care and better nutrition and increased investment in public health matters such as building sewers also helped to lower the infant mortality rate over the two decades. Thus in many respects the period between the wars marks the beginnings of modern America.

2

The Culture of Childhood and Youth

The 1920s was a period of flaming youth, a period when society worshiped and tried to emulate young people, a time when society's heroes were young and on the make. Yet these images were the images of popular culture, of a vast, media-made pattern that had little to do with the real experiences of children and young people. Fewer young people worked in factories during the 1920s than before, even though the two federal child labor laws had been declared unconstitutional. Most children and young people attended school, although the schools in large cities were frequently overcrowded and the teachers overwhelmed by the numbers of students they had to teach. More and more American children now lived in cities. After 1920 the majority of Americans lived in places that could be called urban.[1]

Life in the cities of the early twentieth century was remarkably public. Except for the upper crust, most people spent most of their leisure time on the streets or at public amusements. People living in cramped immigrant tenements or in small apartments did not entertain there. There was no room set aside for entertainment, and if there was a spare room, it was in all likelihood rented out. As a consequence, children, young people, and adults mingled freely in the streets and at public amusements. Schools may have segregated children and youth by age and grade, but home life and leisure time still contained what historian Joseph Kett (in another context) referred to as a broad mingling of ages.[2]

Because many children spent a great deal of time on city streets, earnest reformers worried as they tried to improve society by improving the conditions of life for the nation's children. Reformers were horrified by the images of young children working in dangerous factories and were also concerned about the newsboys (and a few newsgirls) and other youthful vendors who could be found on most downtown street corners. They were appalled when they thought about the messenger boys who worked late at night in the city's worst districts—in saloons, gambling dens, and bordellos.

Children of Hestella Kelley, Greensboro, Alabama (ca. 1936). (Photograph by O. S. Welch, Farm Security Administration [FSA]. National Archives Neg. 16-G-160-1-AAA-Ala-61.)

As if these dangerous occupations were not enough, the reformers also observed armies of children playing on the streets or patronizing the shops and cheap amusements of the city. To most reformers, it seemed as if the children of the poor, especially the immigrant poor, were being brought up in the streets. Thus the reformers sought in a variety of ways literally to get the children off the streets.

Why were the children on the streets? One primary reason was because the streets were interesting, presenting a constantly changing panorama of life. The streets were full of people and action; an observer could learn a great deal about how the city (and life itself) worked simply by paying attention to what happened on the streets.[3]

The streets also represented opportunity: the chance to make some money (and to spend it), to meet friends, to start a game, and to socialize, eavesdrop, or have some fun at the expense of some of the adults who also frequented the streets.

The reformers were little comforted by the idea that children were learning not only economics and politics, but also morals, from the streets. Coming from the safety of respectable middle-class districts, these reformers cum moralists feared for the safety of the street urchins and also feared for the future of the nation's moral fiber. But this view failed to understand how the streets actually worked or that they were extensions of the homes of the people whose dwellings lined them.

The streets, contrary to the reformers' notions, might have been more dangerous, not less, if there had been no adults around, because they could lend a hand if a child needed help. The children themselves would probably have agreed with the reformers, to a point. The reformers disliked the idea of kids and adults in the same unsupervised space; the kids would have liked to remove adults and thereby have more room for their games and frolics. What fun is it to open a hydrant if the grocer complains that you are running off his customers?

Besides, part of the fun of growing up in the city was testing limits and skirting the edge of propriety. Nothing was quite so inviting as a "No Swim-

Three kids on a fence, New York City (1936). Part of a series of photographs entitled "One-Third of a Nation" depicting life in the slums of New York City. (Photographers: Arnold Eagle and David Robbins, Works Progress Administration [WPA]. National Archives Neg. 69-ANP-1-P2329-48.)

The neighborhood—kids in a tenement, New York City (1937). Part of a series of photographs entitled "One-Third of a Nation" depicting life in the slums of New York City. (Photographers: Arnold Eagle and David Robbins, Works Progress Administration [WPA]. National Archives Neg. 69-ANP-1-2329-6.)

ming" sign on a hot summer day, for example—nor nothing nearly as much fun as playing tag in and out of the laundry hanging over the alley or over the roofs to the exasperated complaints of adults whose business or leisure was being disrupted. And stealing shards from the ice wagon, hitching rides, and harassing the horses (though by the twenties horses were becoming rarer) all were part of growing up, even if the adults objected.[4]

Children resented the intrusion of adults into their play space, but when young people were selling something, they eagerly sought out adults as customers. Kids negotiated with some adults, taunted others, and tried to avoid the police, who would not cooperate with young people's efforts to make the street their space. With the advent of the juvenile court and a new definition of juvenile delinquency, children were arrested for a variety of activities that would not have been treated as crimes if the perpetrators were adults. But most kids were quicker than the police and delighted in leading them on merry chases in and out of the neighborhoods that kids knew better than any policeman did.

Child drawing with chalk on sidewalk, New York City (ca. 1937). (Photograph by Helen Levitt, WPA. National Archives Neg. 69-ANP-7-P3028-149.)

Looking at this drama through the lenses of reformers and the rose-colored glasses of nostalgic memory, it is still possible to discern some important social processes at work. Adults had always worried about children who did not seem to have anything important (as defined by adults) to do or who seemed to lack supervision. In the nineteenth century, Charles Loring Brace had gained a national reputation as a reformer by rounding up orphaned children on the city streets and shipping them out west to farm families. That all the children were not orphans, that not all families gave their full consent, and that a number of the children so saved wound up back in their old neighborhoods did not deter later reformers from once again trying to get the kids off the streets.[5]

The streets were, at least some of the time, a world created by children for the children's own purpose. The streets represented a place where children certainly did shape their world according to their own notions of right and wrong and fair play. Their notions were often at variance with prevailing social norms. According to historian David Nasaw,

The children learned in school—and probably at home as well—that gambling was wasteful and sinful, stealing was a crime, money was for saving, and citizens owed allegiance to the law and officials sworn to enforce it. On the streets, however, they observed that lots of kids shot craps or pitched pennies, that stealing from the railroads was as common an afternoon's occupation as stickball, that money was for spending, and that your primary duty was to friends, family and fellow gang members—not the police or the laws they claimed to enforce.[6]

In living and playing on the streets, then, children learned how society actually worked. They learned that the people who claimed to be acting in young people's interests could deprive them of some rights and a considerable amount of freedom and that adults expected children to conform to the adult-designed ideal world, rather than the real world kids saw for themselves. They saw that loyalty to their pals brought them some control over their own world; following all the adult-determined rules was boring and dull.

City children who thumbed their noses at adult interference found themselves the targets of powerful new instruments developed by the state. Chief among these instruments was the juvenile court. The first such court had been founded in Illinois in 1899, although Judge Ben Lindsey of the Denver, Colorado, court claimed to have been running what amounted to a juvenile court even earlier. The idea behind the court was that it would use the parental power of the state (*parens patriae*) to remedy the social ills evidenced by youthful misbehavior and the lack of supervision by natural parents. Earlier efforts to confront the problem—houses of refuge, reform schools, placing-out systems, and the like—had helped, but as the new century dawned, a separate court was created to complete the process of separating youthful offenders from adult convicts. The juvenile court was separate from the adult criminal courts and had much broader jurisdiction. Children who came before the court did not have to be convicted of a crime to fall under the court's jurisdiction; if it found that a child was in need of supervision—the beneficial element of the court process—then that child came under the control of the court. So when kids dodged the police on the streets, they were not only ducking some minor judicial procedure but also trying to avoid gaining a whole new set of adult supervisors.[7]

Not only did the court have broad jurisdiction according to the statutory law that set it up, it also had the prestige of science—specifically the new science of psychology—behind it. William A. Healy, a respected M.D., became the director of the Juvenile Psychopathic Institute (a research and clinical facility associated with the Cook County Juvenile Court in Chicago) in 1909. According to Jane Addams of Hull House, the well-known Chicago settlement, the institute would attempt to find the causes of juvenile delinquency in individual cases and then seek a course of treatment to remedy the problem; that is, delinquency would be studied scientifically and a solution found. By

1915 Healy had published *The Individual Delinquent,* a handbook for juvenile workers, based on cases that had been referred to the institute. Healy reported that there was no single causative factor or theory that explained the origins of juvenile delinquency. Rather, he noted, each case was unique, and thus he could speak only of various "causes" such as "bad companions," "mental conflicts," and "love of adventure."[8]

In the following year, Healy and his assistant, Augusta F. Bronner, presented to a scientific meeting about youthful offenders a paper that stressed the need for a holistic approach to the problem of delinquency. They concluded that "our whole work shows nothing more certainly than that no satisfactory study of delinquents, even for practical purposes, can be made without building sanely upon the foundations of *all* that goes to make character and conduct."[9]

Ironically, Healy and Bronner's commonsense approach to the study of delinquents may well have contributed to the growth of a juvenile justice system that recognized almost no legal limitations on its powers. The court as an institution prided itself on applying individual remedies to individual delinquents. This approach meant that the juvenile court effectively denied due process to the young people who came before it.

In 1917, Healy published another volume, *Mental Conflicts,* arguing that "mental analysis" (Healy's version of psychoanalysis) needed to be added to the holistic approach to juvenile delinquency. Of 2,000 cases studied, Healy found 147 "instances where mental conflict was a main cause of the delinquency." He retained the holistic approach and broadened his views to include early family life (a precursor to a developmental approach) as a causative factor. "Parental relationship," he concluded, "is so vitally connected with the emotional life of childhood [that] the suggestion of irregularity in it comes as a grave psychic shock."[10]

Healy's findings mark the entering wedge into the family and into children's lives of a powerful combination: child science and the juvenile justice (or family court) system. For city kids, the threat of being run in by the police was now double-edged. You could wind up in juvenile court, and the court might refer you to a doctor or a therapist who would try to find out what was wrong with you. The fact that your parents were immigrants and that you came from a different cultural background would not be considered. By being caught "breaking the law" by a policeman, you had already been defined as someone in need of the court's help, so kids posted lookouts and ran when they spotted the police or other suspicious or nosy adults.[11]

Given the various threats to their world, children and young people carried on, earning money by selling papers or other items and spending their earnings on cheap amusements, candy, and other treats. When they were not working, children played improvised games in the streets and on the sidewalks or took part in the more organized games of baseball and stickball played by older boys. These games carved out spaces in a bustling, urban world. Games paused, but only briefly, when traffic interrupted them. Passing adults were not enough to stop a game, and they might find themselves in some danger if a hit came their way. Smaller children kept mostly to the sidewalk and stayed closer to the home stoop than did their older siblings.

Passing streetcars were frequently too tempting to resist, and kids hitched rides (or hung on the outside of the car), much to the dismay of the reformers. Girls tended to stay closer to home than boys because girls were less likely to work at selling papers than their brothers and because many of the girls' duties, such as minding the younger children, kept them in the house. Some girls did sell papers, and some worked after school, but there were never as many girls in the streets as there were boys, and the younger girls did not roam the city the way their brothers did. Older girls, those out of school but still living at home, were a different matter.

Boys had to travel from their school and home neighborhoods to the downtown districts where the buyers were, but they had two hours between the end of school and the end of the workday, so they filled this time with their games and used the streets as their playgrounds. Sometimes the games just seemed to happen. "Kick the can" required only a can and some players. Others were more structured—kids waiting at the distribution point might be shooting craps or pitching pennies or just hanging out. Whatever the kids were doing, the do-gooders looking on wanted to stop it because the congregation of boys having fun made the reformers nervous.

Once the papers were out, the children switched from play to selling, and the adults they had ignored only moments before became the targets of their sales pitches. The newsies sold to people on the way home from work, and they set up in front of subway and trolley stops, at the entrances to department stores, or anyplace where people with change in their pockets gathered. Big headlines greatly assisted sales, and sometimes young sellers were not above exaggerating the paper's contents in order to make a sale.

When they had money, kids knew what they wanted to do with it: spend it. They spent it on cheap amusements, especially lively action motion pictures, various machines in the arcades, or cheap candy that was readily available. Money was power, and kids knew what they wanted; merchants stocked what sold and at prices kids could afford. When reformers tried to convince the movie house managers to show uplifting or educational films, the kids stayed away in droves. They wanted action and excitement, not some adult's idea of what was good for them. So, in a sense, the children of the 1920s shaped the amusements that developed. In this way, they were having an impact on public entertainment, and by extension they were having an impact on the development of mass culture.[12]

By the end of the 1920s, the golden age of the newsies came to an end as some newspapers went to adult vendors and as home delivery in the suburbs cut into city sales. There were still kids selling papers on the streets in the twenties and thirties, but there were not nearly as many as there had been before World War I.

In the neighborhoods and on the streets, children still played their games after school and still dodged in and out of traffic, and reformers still worried about getting the kids off the streets. What the reformers had not noticed was that the children had been effectively structuring their own lives. They played their games according to rules, and they arbitrated disputes fairly if not always quietly. They learned a rough democracy on the streets, and they learned how the world worked by watching it up close. They saw the drinking and gambling that went on in saloons and gambling halls; they not only understood prostitution but may well have known some of the prostitutes. Children's lives were not protected in the way that adults wanted, but kids tried to control their world so that the risks they took were acceptable.[13]

The adult reformers had their own conception of what being a child should mean. The reformers were promoting values very different from those they saw as being epitomized by the behavior of city kids. Reformers were contending for a sheltered childhood populated by what one scholar has called the "economically 'useless' but emotionally 'priceless' child."[14] Children were to be protected not only from abuse and neglect but also from the seamier aspects of life. They were to be nurtured and cherished so that they could live up to their full potential. The future of society depended on it. An army of experts, all focusing on some aspect of growing up, began proffering volumes of advice—much of it confusing and contradictory, but all of it aimed at inadequate parents who had failed to bring up their children properly. Consider, for example, the following comments from Dr. Douglas A. Thom, a Boston psychiatrist writing in 1922:

> The home represents the workshop in which ... personalities are being developed, and the mental atmosphere of the home can be very easily contaminated. The ever-changing moods of the parents, colored by their indifference, their quarrels, depressions, and resentments, and shown by their manner of speech and action, are decidedly unhealthy; so, too, are the timidity of a mother, the arrogance of a father, the self-consciousness of a younger sister, and the egotism of an older brother. Under such conditions we find a mental atmosphere as dangerous to the child as if it were contaminated by scarlet fever, diphtheria, or typhoid.[15]

Other voices chimed in with concerns about the quality and nature of homes in the working-class districts of the city. The evidence for the pathology was the continued presence of large numbers of children on the streets, the continually filled dockets of the juvenile courts, and the resistance of parents to the good advice being peddled by the experts.

The problem was that the experts and the reformers had one vision of childhood and children, whereas working-class parents and children had differing views. Most of the reformers were middle-class in outlook if not in status, whereas most of the young people they wished to change were working-class. Working-class parents had their own concerns. Sometimes they needed the money their children made. As families struggled to survive in the urban world, they certainly needed the sorts of domestic services girls provided. Parents worried less about the danger their sons courted than the danger they as a family courted trying to make a living in the city. And they resented the assumed superiority of the reformers.

Jane Addams saw that young people could not be expected to conform to schoolmarmish notions about proper behavior, but she also argued for the nurturing of youth and for the idea that society should invest in its young people. She would not condemn the liveliness and activities of children, but she did want to give them a better future than their parents could. She sensed that there was something of value in youthful exuberance, but she probably did not understand just how many lessons the young people on the streets were actually learning. When adults set agendas for children, children naturally resist. But resisting does not mean that the children stop learning. It means only that the lessons children learn may not be the ones the adults want them to learn.[16]

The reformers accomplished a great deal for children, despite their failure to understand fully the nature of children's lives and their culture. They helped to make schooling universal; they helped to reduce infant mortality and to promote better access to health care. They began a campaign to eliminate child labor and did succeed finally in ending some of the exploitation of children by large factories. More important, reformers spoke out in a variety of contexts and for a variety of programs, all of which had as their goal the improvement of children's lives. Children may have run from the police on the streets, but they also benefited from the efforts of people who cared about them.

As the twenties gave way to the thirties, some families moved away from the crowded apartments of the inner city, and others moved in to take their places. Kids still sold newspapers on the street, and kids still used the streets and sidewalks as their playgrounds, but there were more supervised playgrounds and more adult-sponsored after-school activities. There were still cheap amusements, arcades, movie theaters, and candy stores near where the kids congregated, but the kids had more money now—or they had less if they were newcomers. Those whose families moved to better neighborhoods probably still had sidewalks and stoops, but they lived in quieter districts that had less excitement and less traffic. Neighborhoods in these newer districts had services and corner stores, but the mix of business and residence that had characterized the older parts of the city no longer prevailed. There were movie theaters in the new areas, too, but they showed films that appealed to whole families instead of audiences of kids. So families improved their lot, and the children went to better, less-crowded schools, but in moving off the diverse urban streets of the early twenties, they lost something, too. They lost some of their ability to control a space and a small amount of time, and they lost the possibility of learning for themselves how life works.

As for the newcomers to the urban districts in the late twenties and in the depression years, they found a city contracting rather than expanding. At first, as the depression deepened, local relief agencies tried to cope with the rising tide of misery in the country, but they were soon overwhelmed and could offer little more than advice. The life of the streets did not dry up, but the sense of possibility of an open and exciting future was gone. And very few kids had any money to spend at all.[17]

Meanwhile the older brothers and sisters of the kids on the streets had left school and entered the world of work and youth. Thousands of young women were employed in the cities. Some worked in factories, some worked in department stores, and some of them worked as telephone operators or secretaries. Some of them were country girls—single young women who had only recently moved to the city—and some were the daughters of families who had come to the city from the countryside or from abroad. Young women met and mingled at work, and after work they looked for amusement and excitement. Most of the girls who lived at home helped to support their working-class families, but they sometimes took money out of their pay- checks to buy clothes or makeup or hats. Sometimes, too, working girls who lived at home found ways to get out at night to meet and socialize with the opposite sex, even though the traditions of their parents were against such behavior. Young women would conspire with their brothers and leave home with an escort and chaperon, being free to be on their own until it was time to go back home together.

The boys, too, had come to the city looking for work or were living at home and, like their sisters, helping out until the family got on its feet. Boys generally had more money than their sisters, and so boys would "treat" the girls they met. A group of girls would go to a dance hall, where they would mingle with the boys who came there. They would dance, have drinks in the adjacent bar, and sometimes the couples would pair off and go on to explore other amusements or retire to a room somewhere. This system of "treats" gave the young women access to the amusements the city offered and allowed the young men to claim sexual favors from the young women.[18]

In the twenties, the movies moved uptown to the central business dis- tricts, where theater managers erected huge palaces to attract a broader and higher-paying audience. Neighborhood theaters where kids and immigrant families could spend their coins persisted, but the big show was downtown and was out of range for many of the street children. But these new theaters attracted a new clientele, young working women. Various estimates in the 1920s put the percentage of women in movie audiences at 60 percent or even higher than 80 percent. For immigrant daughters in particular, the movies provided images of a world totally different from that of their parents. Young women could see titles such as *The Amateur Wife, Why Change Your Wife?* and *Forbidden Fruit*. At the theater, too, they found themselves in a new world, one segregated from the teeming streets. Here there was an elaborately designed interior and handsome young white male ushers to preserve the dignity and purity of the surroundings. African-Americans, provocatively dressed women, and lower-class men were turned away, and those who did not fall into those categories could believe that they fit in and that they belonged.

Of course, many moralists were aghast at the implied immorality of such films. There were many efforts at censorship, but the opponents could not agree about precisely what dangers the movies represented. Consequently, though the moralists raged, and though the movies had toned down after World War I, efforts at censorship in the 1920s came to naught.[19]

The censors were most concerned about what the movies taught about sex. As there were no other public ways to learn about love, romance, sex, and reproduction, the movies presented the younger audience members with what amounted to a primer on how to behave with the opposite sex. One 16-year-old girl admitted that she learned a lot from the movies and what she learned affected her own behavior. "I know love pictures have made me more receptive to love-making because I always thought it rather silly," she wrote, "until these pictures where there is always so much love and everything turns out all right in the end." She concluded by adding, "I kiss and pet much more than I would otherwise."[20]

A major change in youth mores during the twenties was brought about by the development of the culture of dating. Boys would take girls out and pay for an evening's entertainment and amusement. In return the girls provided companionship and, as the custom developed, some petting. The custom of dating regularized the process and eased the pressure on girls to trade sexual favors for an evening's entertainment. Dating had evolved from the system of informal meeting of young people in gathering places and had been made necessary because working-class young people could not carry out the more formal system of courtship. For one thing, the system of courtship required a parlor so that "gentleman callers" might be received. For another, many immigrant families were opposed to the easy informality that had developed between the sexes in American cities. Dating was a way around these difficulties.[21]

Although dating may have regularized the process of socializing between young people, it did not entirely remove pressure for some sort of reciprocity. In May 1922, in Port Huron, Michigan, Mrs. Helen B. Paulson addressed a parent education group sponsored by the local Parent-Teacher Association. "If girls would pay their own way when they go out with young men," she said, " 'petting' would be greatly diminished." She wanted parents to pay more attention. "Oh, if parents only realized the position they are putting their girls in when they let them accept all their good times at the boys' expense!" she continued. "Why often when I've remonstrated with girls about letting their boyfriends take personal liberties with them, they look at me innocently and say, 'Why, what else can we do for them in return for the money they've spent on us.'" Her remedy for this problem was using more corporal punishment and developing in children "the habit of obeying commands."[22]

Moreover, according to historian Beth Bailey, dating "made access to women directly dependent on money." Some young men complained that girls were becoming too expensive, and others pointed out that in effect the women were engaged in a kind of prostitution because they sold their company to their dates. But these complaints probably missed the point. The money the boys and young men had showed their greater social power, or as Bailey puts it: "The regulations that grew up to govern dating codified women's inequality and ratified men's power." And dating was in many respects another form of conspicuous consumption, a way of competing for young men and young women.[23]

Dating became universal among young people, and it continued even during the depression. In a study of working-class and immigrant girls associated with the University Settlement House in Cleveland, the author found that the preferred activity for these teenage women was "dancing," followed closely by "parties with boys" and going to movies. Parties with girls ranked a distant fourth.[24]

Parents worried about the new freedom the dating culture represented, and they worried especially about daughters and sex. When teenage daughters known to be sexually active refused to heed parental warnings or submit to parental discipline, parents sometimes called in the authorities. Juvenile courts were willing in such cases to send stubborn daughters to institutions such as the New York State Reformatory for Women at Bedford Hills. There had been, of course, serious family conflict before the young women were committed. At issue was the family honor and with it the question of the daughter's autonomy and her sexuality. Behind the behavior of girls sentenced to Bedford Hills was usually considerable conflict and unpleasantness in the family, and this sometimes even included sexual abuse of the daughter. Although some social scientists had begun to develop a more sympathetic understanding of the lives and culture of children and youth, the court system and most social agencies continued to enforce an older code of female behavior. Even though some "wayward girls" had been raped and made pregnant against their will, all girls who came to the attention of the courts were lumped into one category and imprisoned because they had been sexually active, regardless of the circumstances.

Once imprisoned, the girls struggled against the authority and coercion of the staff and frequently developed close personal relationships with other inmates. After one year, the girls were paroled, having learned, it was hoped, some sense. Most girls on parole were sent home or to some domestic situation where they were expected to conform to social norms, and their behavior was very closely monitored. Those who violated the terms of their parole were sent back to Bedford.[25]

The 1920s seemed to be a time when sexuality permeated American culture. Certainly sexual themes were a part of a great many movies, and there was a kind of celebration of youthful sexuality among the avant-garde, especially those who were pioneering in social science, but this celebration did not represent the views of most Americans, as the experiences of the young women sent to Bedford Hills illustrate. The discussion of youthful sexuality, especially the celebration of female sexuality, was in large part a reaction against the ideology of Victorian repression, as some of the avant-garde phrased it. Those who wished to glorify the rediscovery of female sexuality (modernizers) were at one extreme of a larger social process—the redefinition of female adolescence—while the courts and most of the more conservative parts of society (traditionalists) were at the other.[26]

Although dating grew out of the working-class social milieu, it was taken up by middle-class youth who attended college and redefined to fit their circumstances. Like the children of the city streets, youth who attended college wished to exercise greater control over their own lives while preserving a sense of belonging to a larger group or set of people. Whereas city children resorted to informal groups and local understandings of turf and hierarchy, college youth had to carve out for themselves a set of understandings that applied to their own circumstances. And they had to do this in a world characterized by rapid changes in the lives and experiences of young people.[27]

Adolescence itself was changing. Young men who could afford higher education could rest in the knowledge that successful completion of college ensured them a place in America's expanding economy. Completion itself was all that mattered; academic excellence was considered odd. Young women now began to claim the same rights to education their brothers had and, by implication, were beginning to think seriously about identities other than that of wife and mother. By leaving home for college or for work, girls had gained an enormous amount of personal freedom. But freedom could also be threatening because the total lack of supervision could be damaging to reputations and future prospects. Some via media had to be found. The rituals of dating, as refined and supported by college fraternities and sororities, filled this need.[28]

Dating spread rapidly across the country in the 1920s and gave rise to a different set of social relations between young people. In substance, the date represented a kind of bargain. Boys paid; girls granted some degree of intimacy. Rules established by the peer group defined the limits and the timing of the relaxation of those limits. According to historian John Modell,

Girls had more to gain by the establishment of dating, because the new version of the double standard that it put into place was considerably less restrictive to them than the one it replaced. Before dating parents had tended to construe strictly girls' obligation to enter marriage untainted by even a hint of scandal, and they supervised courting accordingly, limiting both its occasion and the set of eligibles. The boy who came calling had not only to be prepared to behave himself but he also had to pass *prima facie* muster as a boy who by reputation *would* behave himself.[29]

Youth of the 1920s were at once more liberated than previous generations and more conforming. Peer groups enforced strict rules of conduct and codified the process of rebellion against adult authority. At the same time, peer groups made it possible for young people to experiment with their behavior, including sexual behavior, and learn more about members of the opposite sex through dating relationships. Thus young people were free from close adult supervision of some parts of their lives, but to gain this freedom, they had to sacrifice some elements of individuality. Peer groups made it safe to experiment, but they enforced conformity and a fairly strict "rating and dating" mentality. All was not equal within peer groups; status depended upon qualities such as wealth, personal appearance, social background, and conformity to group rules.[30]

According to Modell, "the 1920s promoted the emergence of our modern youthful life course, normatively sanctioned for the middle class." That is, the pattern that has become commonplace for young people since World War II actually began in the 1920s. Modell describes this pattern as "extended schooling combined with an early and gradual peer-structured courtship system, while promoting an early and often romantic marriage." Modell saw this development as leading to a break between generations and a tendency for new families to be more separate from the families of origin.[31]

Like the peer groups themselves, the rules or norms young people set represented a middle way. Peer group norms permitted petting but not sexual intercourse, and any couple that actually went "all the way" suffered serious sanctions. Pregnant women were disgraced, and men who were responsible for getting their girlfriends pregnant were regarded as cads or worse. Drinking was permitted even though national prohibition was in effect, but drunkenness was considered disgraceful. Fraternities and sororities made it possible for young people to explore their own sexuality and to consume alcohol and tobacco and at the same time protected them from excessive adult supervision.

What adults found threatening about the new mores on college campuses was that the students not only allowed a form of sexual expression but also talked about it. "There are only two kinds of girls," one student editor wrote, "those who have been kissed and those who are sorry they haven't been kissed."[32] Students defended their activities as being normal, and not dangerous. They denied that they were promiscuous or immoral. The rules and limits students set for themselves were enforced through a complex system of "gossip, reference, bull-session discussions, and careful conformity to standards." Within such a system, a coed who had the reputation of being too "fast" or too "easy" could quickly find herself in a social no-man's-land.[33]

The pattern that emerged in the 1920s remained in place in the 1930s, but there was less public concern about it. Petting (the names for this activity varied) was now commonplace and expected. As one college student remarked in the 1930s, "flaming youth has lost its novelty." And what was once novel and notorious on college campuses had become ordinary there but new and remarkable among high school students. Thus college students set the pace, and high schoolers emulated them. Although petting no longer attracted the attention of moralists, the frequency of premarital intercourse increased during the 1930s. Studies of college students in the 1930s found that one-fourth of college women and one-half of the men had engaged in premarital intercourse. Among engaged women, the number who had had intercourse rose to 47 percent, but almost all of those had engaged in coitus only with their intended spouse.[34]

One reason the new behaviors of the 1920s had lost their notoriety by the 1930s was that American concern with public morals had shifted during the decade. The three major reform movements concerned with sexuality all fizzled during the 1920s. The social hygiene movement, which advocated sex education as a defense against sexually transmitted diseases and prostitution, seemed to die out, as did the social purity movement and the birth control movement, which declined as the middle classes came to accept birth control as routine. Female sexuality had come to be accepted, and equally significant, young people had more freedom. One other trend was the decline of prostitution in American cities, a trend probably related to the rising rate of premarital intercourse, especially among engaged couples.[35]

For most children and young people, the depression represented a serious contraction of possibilities and opportunities. Families strained by tightened resources cut back on recreation and the use of automobiles, thereby limiting the freedom young people had enjoyed in the previous decade. More young people sought work in order to help their families, though for many this was an unsuccessful effort. The average age at which couples married rose during the depression, meaning that many young people delayed getting married until their economic circumstances permitted them to do so. This probably contributed to rising rates of premarital intercourse, and this practice provoked a variety of commentary. A national poll asked respondents if the government should provide aid so that engaged couples could marry. Thirty-eight percent said yes.[36]

The experiences of African-American youth, particularly in the South, were profoundly different from those of white youth and also from the lives of African-American youth who grew up in northern cities. Although ethnic differences may have been important at the neighborhood level, the early twentieth century was a time when various European ethnicities blended into the designation of "white," a process that cast African-Americans as "the other," so that people of varying backgrounds could come together. Both regions of the country were segregated—northern public spaces by custom and practice, southern spaces by law. The fact and process of racial segregation influenced all aspects of life. For example, the Social Security Act of 1935 excluded domestic and agricultural workers, most of whom were African-Americans, in order to win the support of southern Democrats for its passage.[37]

In the 1930s, the American Youth Commission, a subunit of the American Council on Education, supported a series of studies of African-American youth. Published in 1940, a study titled *Children of Bondage,* by Allison Davis and John Dollard, focused on the personality development of children in New Orleans, Louisiana, and Natchez, Mississippi. Davis and Dollard found that racial segregation shaped and controlled the lives of children in a variety of ways. They also found that among African-Americans, who the authors believed constituted a caste (that is, a separate and unchangeable subgroup of society), there were several levels or classes, determined by income levels and by behavior.

Children whose parents were at the lowest economic levels grew up in a world of chaos. They were surrounded by people whose lives were characterized by strife and violence. A child's parents were "very likely to separate several times during his life," and extramarital affairs were common, as was fighting. Although churches were available, attendance was spotty, and the messages preached were "the class ways" in which the ethics expounded were "warnings against dancing, card playing, Sunday baseball and 'too much' science and education." In this world, illegitimate births and delinquency were very common. A 15-year-old boy told one of the interviewers that he had failed the fifth grade twice. Whenever he came home from school, he said, his father told him he would never amount to anything and gave him a whipping. Even the discipline was chaotic:

> The source of discipline in a lower class family changes frequently from mother to father to aunt, to grandmother, to uncle or to an older child. But whoever the disciplinarian at any given moment may be, he is certain to believe that the way to make a child learn is to beat him. . . . A lower class mother in New Orleans says of her son of thirteen, "he went out when I told him not to. I tried to choke his neck off when I got him."[38]

As income and education levels rose, the amount of violence around and against children declined, but all African-Americans suffered under a system that allowed no resistance to white control or aggression. Under these circumstances, all African-American children grew up in a society where their choices were limited and the chances of advancement were severely restricted.

Work and self-reliance thus came fairly early to African-American children. It was rare for children to go to school beyond the elementary grades because families gave relatively little support to school attendance and because they needed the income that children could generate. African-American children found jobs at very low rates of pay. Older children might work in service jobs—in restaurants, for example, or, for boys, at various kinds of labor. Younger girls frequently found work as domestics, working as maids or providing child care. In some respects, the experiences of African-American children in the South resembled those of immigrant children in northern cities, but immigrant children never faced the inflexible lines of caste and race that dominated the segregated South.[39]

If the 1920s were the decade of "flaming youth"—at least so far as privileged young people were concerned—in the 1930s, the flame flickered for some and went out entirely for others. In *Children of the Depression,* a massive study of the effects of the depression on family life, sociologist Glen Elder asked what impact the loss of income had had on the lives of children. For example, reduced family circumstances led many children to enter the workforce. Certainly the economic circumstances of many families changed. According to Elder, "a large number of the study members are convinced that hardship in the Depression has made a difference in their financial outlook." In addition, "they tend to use the Depression as an explanation for their behavior." As one young white-collar worker put it, he had come to "realize that money doesn't always come so easy. It makes you just a little conservative in spending money, especially in spending it beyond your means."[40] One study in Michigan found that only 7,500 of an estimated 45,000 high school graduates went on to college. The study recommended that the leaving age for compulsory school attendance be raised from 16 to 18 so that young people could be held out of the job market a bit longer.[41]

European observers were surprised at the passivity of the unemployed in the United States. Radicalism or mob action seemed to have no place, and even in the election of 1932, the Communists polled only 120,000 votes. Despite the apparent passivity, some observers believed that society itself was disintegrating. The birthrate had fallen, and pundits saw a dire future if the trend continued. Schools would stand empty, markets were shrinking, and the means to recover might never be available.[42]

Under these circumstances, society tended to ignore the voice and interests of children and young people, even though the previous decade had been the age of youth. Youth symbolized the future and the bright hope of endless economic expansion. At a time when resources and morale were declining, the same behavior that had made young people the darlings of society now seemed indulgent and wasteful. Elder found that many children reported a return to basic values as a result of the hard times.[43]

Although youth no longer commanded the attention of society as they had in the 1920s, there was still some important concern about young people. At a convention of the newly formed Congress of Industrial Organizations (CIO), the delegates passed the following resolution:

WHEREAS
1. The burden of depression and unemployment has fallen with peculiar weight upon the young men and women of the country who have been deprived of opportunities for education and of the independence which comes with full time employment, and
2. It has been part of the history of reaction in other countries that anti-labor and anti-democratic political and economic forces have been appealed to the discontent of unemployed youth for the purpose of creating anti-democratic movements, therefore be it

RESOLVED:
1. That this convention express deep concern with the fate of the younger generation;
2. That it endorses the New Deal measures designed to aid youth, such as the NYA, CCC camps, and the WPA and calls for their continuation and extension under civilian control; and
3. That it asserts the willingness of the CIO to collaborate and cooperate with all youth organizations and movements whose object is to secure the loyalty of young people to democracy and progress.[44]

Clearly one of the reasons for interest in youth in the 1930s was a concern about the rise of fascism in Germany and a fear that a similar movement might develop in the United States.

In 1939, a chapter of the Young Communist League at the University of Michigan claimed to have 80 members. The chapter published its own newsletter, *Left Review,* and in May 1939 was still following the party line. "Our activity as YCLers," read one editorial, "has always helped to build the democratic front, but we must make sure that the activity of League members is always that activity which, in every instance, does the *most* to build the democratic front." One project of the league was an effort to raise consciousness about racism in Ann Arbor. A column noted that several restaurants on State Street had refused to serve African-Americans. "The abolition of Jim Crow policies in Ann Arbor," the *Left Review* trumpeted, "will come from a united effort by all progressives who realize that they are attacks upon democracy and therefore a threat to all."[45]

The depression magnified the differences in class. Young people from affluent families found their lives relatively unchanged; those in the lower reaches of the middle class saw their circumstances constrict the most; and youth from lower-class families experienced hardship, but not a loss of status.

One indicator of this change could be found in the patronage of child guidance clinics. Originally intended to prevent delinquency in lower-class youth,
these clinics shifted their focus to emotional problems and by the 1930s
catered to a middle-class clientele.[46]

This shift reflected a widespread expansion of services to, and concern
about, youth during the thirties. Most colleges offered courses in marriage
and family life, and many high schools also offered similar classes. Counseling, once stigmatized and associated with social problems, now became
widely available for the middle classes and on college campuses.[47]

As family resources dried up, young people found that they could not
afford the usual recreation activities such as going to the movies or out on a
date. According to an observer at the time, "the home environments were
such that they did not care to entertain their friends in their homes." As a
result, "the young men contented themselves in hanging around corners, creating mischief, and in general hell-raising to break the monotony of their dull
lives." This certainly led to concern by the authorities. Girls tended to stay
home, where they contributed to the family economy by sewing, and they
amused themselves by "reading cheap magazines." Most youth agencies were
"unprepared for the hoard [sic] of unemployed recreation seekers."[48]

Youth's star had risen in the 1920s, and it pulled younger children along
with it. The personal freedom of both children and youth expanded, and they
took advantage by gaining more influence over the spaces where they played
or engaged in recreation. Self-appointed moralists continued to worry about
young people, especially about the apparent decline in morality represented
by the increasing talk in public about sex and sexuality and the declining
supervision of children and youth. In one sense, children and youth had more
freedom—children on the streets after school and youth once away from the
eyes of their parents—but in another, that freedom was curtailed both by peer
groups and by the schools' expanding hold on the lives of students. When the
twenties gave way to the depression-bound thirties, youth experienced further constraints. They had less money and so had less access to amusements
and recreation; they still exercised control over the streets and there played
games that required fewer resources. Older youth put off going to college or
gave up the idea completely. Those who did go found the social scene somewhat subdued. Dating continued, but the big parties were less frequent.
Steady dating and engagements became more common. Although many social
agencies dealing with children were seriously constrained during the depression years, some services, such as guidance and family life education, actually
increased. And by the end of the decade, everyone was worried about young
people, so much so that the 1940 White House conference was entitled
"Children and Youth in a Democracy."[49]

3

Schools and Colleges

Between the wars, schools and colleges grew on a number of fronts. There were more schools, and they expanded their curricula and the number of grades they offered. College and high school enrollments boomed, and school attendance became the common experience of virtually all Americans, whereas college attendance increasingly became the experience of most middle-class Americans. Schools had a number of social functions: they trained children in American values; they taught the principles of order and regularity; they transmitted basic skills; and they brought a substantial number of American children and youth under state-run bureaucratic control.

Most Americans applauded and supported this expansion of public service, regarding schools as both a good social investment because they helped to produce order and regularity in society and also a necessary first step to full participation in society. As American society and the American economy became more complex, the need for more education grew. Business and industry required an educated workforce. Young people seeking work and opportunity could not compete effectively without an adequate educational background, so they went to school. More and more of them stayed in school and stayed longer than their parents or any previous generation. Everyone, it seemed, had a reason to support the expansion of schools and colleges. In many respects, the schools, like other social agencies for children, were the legacies of the Progressive Era before World War I. The institutions the Progressives had established and supported continued in the period between the wars even though Progressivism itself faded.[1]

The raw numbers testify to the terrific increases in school attendance. In 1920 the average daily attendance in public schools was slightly higher than 16 million. By 1930 the number had climbed to more than 21 million, and in 1940 the total stood at 22 million. School enrollment itself had gone from 23 million to 28 million. In that same period, the population had increased from

Rural school children, northern Michigan (ca. 1936). (Photographer unknown. Bentley Historical Library, Ann Arbor, Michigan, Children's Fund Papers, Box 24.)

106 million to 132 million. These numbers represented other changes. At the beginning of the period, 77.8 percent of the population aged 5 to 17 was in school; by 1940, the percentage had risen to 85.3. There were more than 300,000 high school graduates in 1920, or about 16.8 percent of the 17-year-old population. By 1940 there were 1.2 million graduates, or 50.8 percent of the 17-year-old population. School terms had increased from an average of 161.9 days in 1920 to an average of 175 days in 1940.[2]

Another way of looking at the increase in school attendance is to note that of the young people born between 1905 and 1909 (who would reach age 17 between 1922 and 1926), about 35 percent graduated from high school. Of those born 10 years later, about 43 percent graduated from high school, and of those born in 1920 to 1924 (who would reach age 17 between 1937 and 1941), more than 50 percent graduated from high school. The same increase held true for college graduates as well. Of those born from 1905 to 1909, about 7 percent eventually graduated from college. Of those born from 1920 to 1924, 9.5 percent graduated from college. It is noteworthy that

Play center, interior of a rural school, northern Michigan (ca. 1936). (Photographer unknown. Bentley Historical Library, Ann Arbor, Michigan, Children's Fund Papers, Box 24.)

despite the devastating impact of the depression, school enrollments and graduation rates continued to increase in the 1930s.[3]

These numbers represent a major transformation in American life. In the years before World War I, college attendance—let alone graduation—was a relative rarity, a privilege reserved for the sons (and a few daughters) of the elite. By the eve of World War II, the privilege had broadened considerably, though it should be noted that few children from the poorest segments of American society attended college. Thus the increase in college enrollments came principally from the middle classes. This was possible in part because family incomes rose faster than college costs during the period. Another important factor in this expansion was a changing perception of the role of college. Nineteenth-century colleges had included large preparatory departments because high schools were not very common. By the 1930s, many colleges were able to drop their preparatory departments because of the greater number of high schools. This in turn allowed the colleges to expand their enrollments of undergraduate students, and the expansion reflected a grow-

Interior of a rural school, northern Michigan (ca. 1936). (Photographer unknown. Bentley Historical Library, Ann Arbor, Michigan, Children's Fund Papers, Box 24.)

ing belief that college attendance was a normal expectation of middle-class young men and young women.[4]

One reason for these dramatic increases was the widespread use of legislation to compel school attendance and thereby to reduce child labor. But more was at stake. Reformers also wished to reshape the nature of American society, and to do so, they believed that they had to gain control of children. This, of course, was not a new insight but came from the experience the federal government had had with Native American children. In the nineteenth century, well-meaning reformers had concluded that Indian children had to be schooled in the ways of civilization and the American republic. Tribal ways—indeed the whole Native American culture—had to be stamped out, and American citizens created. In addition to the program of giving plots of land to individual Indians under the auspices of the Dawes Act, the government also relied heavily on boarding schools, where the emphasis was heavily vocational. Boarding schools were thought to be an ideal way of accomplishing the goal of assimilation because the children could be totally removed from parental influence.

Once in the boarding schools, Indian students found themselves sub-
jected to a military system of discipline in a curriculum emphasizing work.
Physical punishments for offenders were common. Conditions in the boarding schools, as revealed in the Merriam Report of 1928, were deplorable, and
some of the abuses were addressed in the Wheeler-Howard Act of 1934 (the
so-called Indian New Deal), which sought to restore some tribal government.[5] The following reminiscence of a meal at a Canadian school typifies the
circumstances that prevailed in the Indian boarding schools:

> Silently we filed into the refectory, which, from the state of the furnishings
> and settings, was a more appropriate term than "dining room." There were sixteen
> long tables of an uncertain green flanked by benches of the same green. On each
> table were eight place settings, consisting of a tin pie plate, a tablespoon and a
> chipped granite cup. In the middle were two platters of porridge, which, owing to
> its indifferent preparation, was referred to as "mush" by the boys; there were also
> a box of containing sixteen slices of bread, a round dish bearing eight spoons of
> lard (Fluffo brand) and a huge jug of milk. It was mush, mush, mush, sometimes
> watery, with monotonous regularity every Monday, Wednesday, Friday, and Satur-
> day. The boys would have vastly preferred the Boston baked beans that, along with
> a spoonful of butter, were served on Tuesdays, Thursdays and Saturdays.
>
> Not until we had said grace—"Bless this mush," some boys said in secret, "I
> hope it doesn't kill us"—could we begin. But no matter how indifferent the qual-
> ity, no boy, to my recollection, ever refused his portion of mush. During the meal
> there was little conversation except for the occasional "Pass the mush" or "Pass the
> milk" and the clatter of spoons which served as knives and forks as well.[6]

The Merriam Report did lead to some improvements in the diet at Indian
boarding schools, but the depression impacted most Native Americans
severely. As a consequence, hard-pressed parents who had earlier resisted
efforts of the Bureau of Indian Affairs to take their children to the boarding
schools now sent them willingly because they lacked the means to feed and
clothe them adequately. Ironically, just when Native American families began
to use the boarding schools for their own purposes, the government started
closing them—as the Merriam Report had recommended. In 1928, when the
report was published, there were 77 Indian boarding schools with a total
enrollment of about 21,000. By 1941 the number of boarding schools had
been reduced to 49 with an enrollment of 14,000.[7]

Significantly, the pattern devised to acculturate Native American children
was the model for the same process for immigrant children. Progressive
reformers saw the schools as ideal instruments for the "Americanization" of
immigrant children—or for children who came from poor or working-class
homes. Schools would thus help create new standards of behavior and sensibility as well as broader understandings of the basic skills in reading, writing,
and calculation. Schools would also help immigrant children adjust to American life. Poorer families tended to have a more communal approach to the

problems of life and thus tended to place less emphasis on individual development. To leave this pattern untouched would leave an old-world, un-Ameri-
can culture intact. Immigrant culture, like the culture of Native Americans,
would have to be undermined and eliminated.[8]

Schools taught English by the "sink-or-swim" method. Students went to
school; instruction was in English. Students either learned the language or
left. The schools themselves were in poor condition and often immensely
crowded. Teachers were often overwhelmed and thus took out their frustra-
tions on students. Most former students recalled their teachers as cold,
unfriendly, and harsh. Public humiliation was a standard way of controlling
student behavior. Physical punishments were also common. Some girls, who
had tended to be quiet and well behaved, recalled their teachers in a more
favorable light. But students agreed that schools sought to teach more than
basic skills. Schools consciously tried to inculcate a middle-class morality and
sensibility through their curricula. Children were punished or humiliated for
not using proper forms of address, and they were subject to routine inspec-
tions for lice or other health problems.[9]

Schools did not rely on subtlety or sympathy for immigrant culture. Classes
in home economics were established to teach girls how to prepare American-
style dishes and to keep house according to middle-class standards. The ideas
taught in school led to frequent conflicts between girls and their mothers at
home. Sometimes the recipes taught at school mixed dairy and meat products
or used pork, thus violating the kosher practices of Orthodox Jews.[10]

While girls took classes in home economics, boys were enrolled in work-
shops of various kinds. That much of the education offered to immigrant children was vocational stuck most middle-class Americans as appropriate, even
progressive. Parents often welcomed such classes because they led to jobs,
which the poor families often desperately needed. At the same time, the class
basis for such vocational instruction meant that schools were not so much a
means for upward mobility as they were a path to an entry-level job. Mobility
could follow, but the attributes of middle-class culture would have to come
later. In some respects, there was an inherent contradiction in that schools
were supposed to be socializing immigrant and working-class children into
middle-class norms. That much was certainly so, but proper manners and
behavior were one thing, and taking college preparatory classes in high school
was quite another. In effect, the schools spoke with a forked tongue; they
wanted middle-class manners from all children, but they also operated to preserve class and race privilege by channeling immigrant, minority, and working-class children into vocational curricula.[11]

School leaders came to understand that if they wanted to change the lives
of their students, get them off the streets, and create a national culture
through schooling, they would have to provide some additional services
specifically for immigrant children. So sink-or-swim gave way to programs

designed so that children would not sink. Special English classes were one such service; medical examinations—designed in part to prevent some illnesses and to foster increased health consciousness on the part of students and parents—were another. Classes for slow learners also appeared, and over the course of the 1920s, the percentage of immigrant children labeled as retarded decreased as more programs began to cater to their needs.[12]

One way immigrant families defended themselves against the vigorous "Americanization" campaigns of the public schools was to send their children to the parochial schools established by Catholic parishes in most larger cities. These schools usually had a distinct ethnic identity and thus allowed children to preserve not only their home language but also most of their culture and religion. There were Irish, Italian, Polish, and German Catholic parish elementary schools in many cities. Secondary schools tended to be sponsored by several parishes or the diocese. In the 1920s, this pattern began to change as the cost of maintaining schools increased and as the public schools expanded. In most parish schools at that time, instruction was in English (as it was in virtually all the secondary schools). Catholics began to move away from the ethnically identified parish school to a national system of Catholic education that focused more on religion than on ethnicity.[13]

During the Progressive Era, Jewish leaders in New York City began to discuss the possibility of creating a coherent citywide system of Jewish education. In 1910 Mordecai Kaplan and Bernard Cronson surveyed the educational situation and concluded that the demand for Jewish education was small but also that the resources available were even smaller. They estimated that only about one-fifth of the 200,000 Jewish children in the city were receiving any kind of Jewish education and so proposed a centralized effort. But such an effort foundered in its inability to satisfy the various elements of the New York Jewish community. Reformist Jews disliked the Zionist tendencies of some of the leadership, and Orthodox Jews disliked any hint of modernism.[14]

During the 1920s and 1930s, public schools retained much of the reform sentiment that had characterized them in the Progressive Era, but they began to rely more on social science to justify their curricula and many of their policies. One of the goals of the schools was to gain control of children—that is, to remove them from parental control—and then to promote a kind of modern individualism. This process, which was part of the larger cultural movement toward the separation of individuals from their families of origin, was one of the fundamental goals of the schools, but experience taught teachers and administrators that there were significant differences between children, even within various ethnic groups. Seeking to divide children in some way other than by ethnicity, educators wanted to group students by ability and to prescribe educational treatments based on the students' relative ability levels. The development of intelligence testing furnished the answer to this dilemma.[15]

Schools were quick to learn about the intelligence tests given to draftees during World War I, and some districts such as Oakland, California, quickly pressed the tests into use. Meanwhile Stanford psychologist Lewis Terman, the principal proponent of intelligence tests, had suggested that every child should take a mental test and that these tests could be used to reorganize schools along more rational lines. In 1922 he published *Intelligence Tests and School Reorganization,* in which he advocated a curriculum based on a system of classification derived from intelligence test results. Schools liked the tests because they shifted blame for poor performance from the schools to the students. A low test score indicated—so school authorities and test promoters claimed—a lesser ability to learn. Thus students could be classified according to their innate abilities and assigned to appropriate levels of work. Such a system of classification implied a more rationally organized system of schools, and that in turn implied a much more bureaucratic and specialized administrative organization of the schools.[16]

Another legacy of Progressivism, corollary to the idea that immigrant children needed to be assimilated, was the idea that experts, relying on their professional expertise, were the ones to do it. Nowhere was this idea held with more fervor than in the educational establishment. Educational experts, following the lead of large corporations, would rationalize their operations, creating a school system in the process, and they would do this using the very latest scientific and management expertise. The goal of the schools would be to determine winners and losers, and the means of doing this would be the newly developed standardized tests. Schools could use the tests, and the tests alone, to determine the winners and could say that the winners deserved their newly won privileges, such as college admission, because the system recognized and rewarded merit. That the meritorious seemed to be mostly white and middle class was seen as proof that the system worked exactly as it was supposed to.[17]

Among the leaders in the emerging professionalization of school administration, Ellwood P. Cubberly of Stanford stands out because he so clearly stated what he thought the goals of schooling should be—the sorting of students into appropriate categories as a means of improving society. An unabashed elitist, he believed that genetic background explained social failure, and he assumed that African-Americans were inferior and should therefore be segregated. He nonetheless labored vigorously to promote the idea of educational systems, incorporating into his textbooks many of the new school reforms of the period, including vocational guidance, junior high schools, junior colleges, and school hygiene programs.[18]

The education establishment was probably best represented by an informal—though highly influential—organization, the Cleveland Conference, a group that began in 1915 as a result of a survey of the Cleveland public schools. Among the early members were Cubberly, James R. Angell, Abraham

Flexner, Paul B. Monroe, and Edward L. Thorndike, another apostle of testing like Terman. The dominant figure of the Cleveland Conference was
Charles Judd, an educational consultant who believed that a thorough reorganization of the entire educational system was in order. At issue was whether
schools would be controlled locally and as result address primarily local concerns, or whether some sort of national standards for education could be
developed and implemented.[19]

Consistent with trends in business and industry, a national educational
establishment developed. High-profile faculty members together with state
educational bureaucrats and powerful superintendents constituted an educational elite that shaped policies, determined the placement of students, and
more or less controlled the direction of the American education system. Many
of these "administrative progressives," who believed in reform from the top
down, drew their inspiration from the gospel of scientific management as
practiced in American corporations. The education reformers adopted the
elite-board and expert-manager form of governance; they accepted the idea
that the superintendent should have voluminous information at his disposal
(there were very few women superintendents); they used a budgeting process
similar to those that most businesses used; and they sought to rationalize the
educational process so that the final product (graduated students) satisfied
public demands. Thus American education became "national" in the sense that
most school systems had similar structures and related to the public in similar
ways. Most students in most urban school systems had similar experiences
regardless of where they lived.[20]

When Robert S. and Helen Lynd (two well-known sociologists—their
Middletown is an American classic) studied Muncie, Indiana, in the 1920s,
they commented on the importance the community placed on education. In
1925, for example, 45 percent of the city's total expenditures went for
schools. About 70 percent of the young people between the ages of 6 and 21
were in school during the daytime, and others attended a variety of night
classes. The city had continually extended the ages to which its compulsory
attendance laws applied and at the same time extended the school year as
well. The city also extended the programs the schools offered, especially high
school. In 1890 there were 170 pupils in high school, 8 percent of the total
school enrollment. By the 1923–1924 school year, enrollment had reached
1,849, more than a tenfold increase, and now stood at 25 percent of total
school enrollment. The percentage of high school graduates who then
enrolled in college likewise climbed in the same period.[21]

The Lynds found the relationship between education and the American
economy also worthy of comment.

The school, like the factory, is a thoroughly regimented world. Immovable seats in
orderly rows fix the sphere of activity of each child. For all, from the timid six-

year-old entering for the first time to the most assured high school senior, the general routine is much the same. Bells divide the day into periods. For the six-year-olds the periods are short (fifteen to twenty-five minutes) and varied; in some they leave their seats, play games and act out make-believe stories, although in "recitation periods" all movement is prohibited. As they grow older the taboo on physical activity becomes stricter, until by the third or fourth year practically all movement is forbidden except the marching from one set of seats to another between periods, a brief interval of prescribed exercise daily, and periods of manual training or home economics once or twice a week. There are "study periods" in which children learn "lessons" from "textbooks" prescribed by the state and "recitation periods" in which they tell an adult teacher what the book has said.

This factory-like regimen changed as the students continued in school. "With high school comes some differences." There the Lynds found "more 'vocational' and 'laboratory' work." Yet much of the high school routine used "the lesson-text-book-recitation method. In high school classes, for nearly an hour the teacher asks questions and pupils answer then a bell rings." What happened next indicated that the schools had not succeeded in driving the life out of their students. When the bell rang,

> on the instant books bang, powder and mirrors come out, there is a buzz of talk and laughter as all the urgent business of living resumes momentarily for the children, notes and "dates" are exchanged, five minutes pass, another bell, gradual sliding into seats, a final giggle, a last vanity case snapped shut, "In our last class we had just finished"—and another class is begun.

The Lynds saw in this process further evidence of the community's commitment "to endow its young with certain essential supplements to the training received in the home."[22]

In Gary, Indiana, as in Middletown, the schools were the object of community pride and characterized by both stability and expansion. William Wirt, the longtime superintendent, provided stability and became a prominent community figure in the 1920s, serving as a director of the YMCA and as a member of the Council of the Gary Boy Scouts. Like his Middletown counterparts, Wirt stressed the usefulness of the schools as agents of control in the city. He believed that the schools could do a better job of supervising the leisure time of young people than could some of the volunteer agencies, but in his view, it was difficult for the schools to become involved because other agencies had preempted the field. He encouraged cooperation between the schools and the Boy Scouts, bringing them into the school program, aided no doubt by his close association with the scouts.[23]

The Gary schools were already nationally famous because of the system of work, study, and play, sometimes called the platoon system, that Wirt had developed. Under this program, schools were in use day and night and combined both educational and recreational facilities. Evening classes for adults complemented the daytime programs for children. Additionally, the curriculum included a strong vocational element for students older than age 16. These ideas, requiring fairly large physical plants, proved very appealing over the decades after the first such building, the Emerson School, opened in 1909. In 1911, an article written for *Hampton's Magazine,* a popular monthly, gave national attention to the plan, stressing the close relationship between the schools and the business community (chiefly, U.S. Steel), noting the "scientific management" principles common to both and the schools' program of Americanization. An attractive and economical feature of the plan was the continuous use of the school buildings, leading to the label the "platoon plan."[24] Critics of the plan found it too much like a factory, too industrial, even though during the 1920s the workings of industrialism were being hailed as the model for school organization and administration.[25]

In Gary, enrollments continued to grow during the 1920s. The segregated schools for African-Americans were especially crowded. The black population of Gary grew from 1,100 in 1920 to more than 4,000 in 1930, and the number of school-aged African-American children increased from 634 to 2,759 in the same period. The question of segregation was complicated in Gary. White racists supported segregation, and African-American voices seemed divided, some favoring fully integrated schools and others, especially the local chapter of the Universal Negro Improvement Association, the organization headed by Marcus Garvey, advocated separation and racial pride. For most African-Americans, whatever their views on segregation, the quality of the schools their children attended was a major issue. The Gary chapter of the NAACP pushed for integrated schools, whereas in New York City, the NAACP pointed with pride to the fully segregated schools of Harlem. The difference was that all schools in New York had the same standards, and the staff hiring practices were "color blind." Gary schools were segregated by policy rather than by the racial characteristics of the neighborhoods the schools served.[26]

African-Americans in Gary complained to Indiana state officials about the schools, but the state officials simply referred them back to Superintendent Wirt. In 1927, 18 African-American students were transferred to the previously all-white Emerson School. The white students walked out in protest, parading through the streets. The dispute was settled when a new, temporary black school was planned. The African-American community united in opposition, and the local chapter of the NAACP filed suit against the city, charging that an appropriation for a temporary African-American school was illegal. The council rescinded its appropriation, and matters calmed down until several African-American students were transferred from the Emerson School to an older building. Their parents filed suit but finally lost before the Indiana Supreme Court in 1931. At the end of the 1920s, Gary's schools were still segregated.[27]

One aspect of Gary's plan, the teaching of industrial skills by unionized workers, gradually fell into disuse in the mid-1920s, paralleling the decline of vocational education in Sommerville, Massachusetts, and other cities. Industrial jobs were plentiful in Gary, and manual training for boys seemed superfluous. The training in clerical skills the girls received was, by contrast, much more successful because most girls got jobs as a result of their training. As the 1920s came to an end, the schools in Gary were still the center of much of the life of the community, and they provided a wide variety of services, including free medical and dental examinations for all students. Dental work for school children was free.[28]

The high school, a relatively new institution, seemed less regimented than the elementary schools. The curriculum was also more varied. The older tradition of high school focused on the preparation of an educated person, but by the twenties, courses that taught specific skills needed by businesses had become more common. The civic leaders of Middletown were especially proud of these courses because they seemed practical, rather than frivolous. They had almost as much support in the community as the high school basketball team had, that is, nearly universal support among the male business booster types.

The vocationally oriented, skill-based courses that stimulated so much community pride were for the young men in high school, whereas home economics classes presumably served the needs of the young women. These classes taught more traditional homemaking skills, such as baking and canning, but tended to overlook, or give less emphasis to, efficient consumption of ready-made articles. In 1925 a class in child care was added to the curriculum of one of the grade schools, "the first and sole effort on the part of the community to train women for this fundamental child-rearing function."[29]

If there were a watchword for education in the 1920s in Middletown, it was probably efficiency. Because of the presence of a teachers' college in Middletown, there was considerable pressure on the local school system to adopt scientific practices and measurements. The administration of the schools became the province of specialists rather than veteran teachers, and the size and expansion of school systems, including school buildings, were the basis for competition between cities. These developments replicated on the local level what the Cleveland Conference had proposed.[30]

One of the innovations favored by the educational establishment was the junior high school, a separate institution that bridged the gap between the elementary grades and the more individualized curricula of urban high schools. In Sommerville, Massachusetts, the school committee had maintained both a high school and a separate vocational school since 1913. By 1920 it was clear that few students were being attracted to the vocational school, and a similar trend was also happening in nearby Fitchburg, Massachusetts. Instead of going to the vocational school, many students were using the newly created junior high school. The idea behind the junior high school, an institution much discussed in educational reform literature, was that in addition to being a bridge to high school and a time for the transition from childhood to adolescence, the school could provide a certain amount of training in business-oriented skills. One reason this project looked so attractive was that it could extend the time in school for many children, thereby raising the educational level of the workforce. Sommerville began the creation of its junior high school, one of the first in the country, in 1914, when the seventh and eighth grades of Forster Elementary School were separated from the lower grades and given "high school type" classes.[31]

The curriculum choices made by junior high students gave some indication as to why the vocational school was declining. Two-hundred nineteen out of 261 students at Forster Intermediate School chose either the preparatory or the business course, leaving the remainder divided between household and manual arts. Students, or more likely their parents, did not see themselves as going to school in order to take up manual or domestic work. In some respects, this trend frustrated the hopes of the school planners in Sommerville. They had envisioned the junior high school as a kind of sorting mechanism whereby the increased population of the city could be placed in appropriate educational tracks. Almost everyone, it turned out, had more ambition than the school committee had anticipated.

Yet the problems the junior high school solved were far more important than the earlier hopes of the committee. The Forster experiment was so successful that in 1916 the school committee decided to set up a total of four junior high schools. Junior high schools cut the dropout rate and gave a focus to the school life of early adolescence that the graded elementary schools had lacked. That junior high schools did not channel more students into low-status work was of minor consequence.

The war years led to lowered attendance in the Sommerville schools, particularly in the upper grades, as students left to take jobs in the expanding economy. After the war ended, students returned in great numbers, leading to overcrowding. At the same time, an increase in juvenile delinquency aroused public concern both locally and nationwide, and the Commonwealth Fund prepared to establish child guidance clinics to combat the rising tide of youthful misbehavior. In Sommerville the school committee proposed to spend $1 million to enlarge the junior high school buildings.

The proposal led to a two-year controversy revealing that support for the junior high schools came from middle-class immigrants, whereas opposition came from longtime Yankee residents. School-based parent-teacher organizations supported the expansion, but wealthier taxpayers opposed it. The elite even went so far as to propose abolishing the junior high schools and building a new vocational school. A vote to do this passed the board of aldermen by a substantial margin, the reasoning being that the junior high schools were too "progressive" and were thus also too "permissive." The school committee voted unanimously to oppose the motion to abolish the junior high schools.

Eventually, aroused public opinion convinced the board of aldermen to change their stance (a tour of the crowded buildings helped), and in 1921 the aldermen agreed to construct two new junior high school buildings.

The overwhelming popularity of the junior high schools in Sommerville indicated the importance that parents—especially immigrant parents—placed on schools. Parents saw the schools as presenting their children with opportunities for advancement. Vocational schools seemed to be appropriate only for students who had no ambition or who lacked the ability to gain additional education. Thus such schools were not attractive to many parents who were on the move socially and economically and who wanted better schools for their children. Parents who sent their children to Catholic schools were happy with the junior high schools because they prepared their children for entry into the high school world. Schools were an item of community pride, especially in the early 1920s. To oppose schools was to label oneself as being opposed to progress, social improvement, and democracy. Only a few people risked that label, even in the politically conservative 1920s.[32]

Returning to Middletown 10 years later, the Lynds found that the effects of the depression on high school enrollments varied. After a drop in 1928–1929 and another in the following year, high school enrollments began to rise. Increases continued until the 1934–1935 school year, when enrollments again fell, but not back to the 1929–1930 level (the population of Middletown also fell in the same period, perhaps accounting for the decline in high school enrollments). Economic conditions improved somewhat in 1935, and this may also have explained why some students left school in search of work. Enrollments rose again in 1936, even though the city's population showed almost no increase.

The pattern for Gary schools replicated the one for Middletown. High school enrollments rose during the 1930s, largely because a number of teenagers who might have dropped out in better times remained in school. Enrollment in high school grew from 5,000 to 6,000, and the number of graduates went from 500 to 1,000. In 1933 the school budget was cut by one-third (down from $3 million to $2 million). Summer school and night programs were reduced, as were funds for improvement and upkeep. Salaries were reduced by 20 percent; the school year was cut back from 10 months to 9; and all staff had to take a month's vacation in the summer without pay. These cuts were gradually restored as tax revenues slowly crept upward; for example, the 10-month school year returned in 1936. Another effect of the depression was the increase of vocational classes. The African-American community in Gary grew slowly in the 1930s, and their children continued to attend segregated schools. The community remained divided about the issue of segregation. The Gary schools weathered the depression, though not without considerable cost in programs and staff morale, but their story was not significantly different from other school stories around the nation.[33]

During the early years of the depression, the number of students going to college from Middletown fell, although nationally college attendance continued to rise during the depression. Despite this trend, some people began to question the value of college, and the Lynds quote a parent as saying: "I think we've been kidding ourselves in breaking our backs to send our children to college. There just aren't enough good jobs to take care of all the college graduates."[34]

In Middletown fewer young men went on to college during the depression than in earlier years, whereas the number of young women who went to college held steady. The Lynds suggest that this was because more jobs that did not require a college degree were open to young men than to young women. The one occupation widely open to young women was teaching, and by the 1930s, teaching required a four-year degree in many states. Another factor that may have figured in the choices made by young women was that going to college also meant a greater chance of finding a mate. Looked at another way, the decline in college attendance by young men also probably meant that opportunities for social mobility had become more limited because of the depression.[35]

The Middletown schools created a department of research and embarked on a 10-year plan to improve the schools in 1927–1928. Improvement was to be based on a new philosophy that emphasized the individual child. In 1933 the Department of Educational Research of the Middletown schools spelled out the new philosophy:

> Ours is a new philosophy. It advocates that the aim of education should be to enable every child to become a useful citizen, to develop his individual powers to the fullest extent of which he is capable, while at the same time engaged in useful and lifelike activities. . . . We believe in the doctrine of equal educational opportunity for every child to develop according to his abilities, interests, and aptitudes.[36]

This philosophy and the use of a planning technique developed in industry underscored the degree to which schools had become centralized and bureaucratized. The philosophy also indicated the degree to which the administrative apparatus had come to rely on standardized tests. These were not mere sentiments. In 1930 a new curriculum was adopted at Central High School that was supposed to be based on the needs of individual students rather than the "one-size-fits-all" approach of the previous curriculum. As a consequence of this new philosophy, students would now see guidance counselors at least once each semester.

The original purpose of the guidance counselors was to help students plan for future employment, but as the system was put into place, counselors found that they spent more time discussing personal problems than vocational or academic ones. Parents' reactions were mixed, some regarding counseling as another costly frill that wasted taxpayers' money. School administrators needed the program, though, because of the rise in enrollments and because of the variety of courses now offered in the high school. A teacher lamented the lack of time characteristic of the new system, resulting in a lack of time to see students. Specialization of function had come to Central High School, too.[37]

Just as schools had grown in the 1930s, college enrollments burgeoned in the early twentieth century, tripling between 1900 and 1930. The growth in college enrollments was especially pronounced in the 1920s; by 1930, about 20 percent of the college-aged population was enrolled. As college enrollments rose, fascination with the world of youth and its behavior also expanded, creating the cult of "flaming youth" in the 1920s. The interest in, and focus on, youth reflected both the rise of advertising directed at the youth market and the rise of national media attention. College students and their scandalous doings were national news, and merchants directed their advertising at youth and used their images to sell products.[38]

The growing enrollments in colleges and universities effectively transformed them from bastions of elite privilege into popular institutions. This expansion not only transformed the role of colleges and universities in American society but also provided the location for the development of the cult of youth and the rising importance of the peer society. The most active peer groups were to be found on the campuses of coeducational colleges, such as large state universities or large and complex private institutions. Administrators worried about the impact that rising enrollments would have on their institutions. Smaller, elite, same-sex institutions began to limit their enrollments in the 1920s so that they could maintain their character and exclusivity—primarily by trying to keep down the number of Jewish students. In the 1930s, elite women's colleges began talking about their "Jewish problem" and began severely restricting enrollments. Radcliffe, for example, consistently admitted about two-thirds of all applicants but limited Jewish women to between 16.5 and 24.8 percent of all Jewish applicants.[39]

According to historian Paula Fass, student life at the colleges revolved around three foci: the formal academic structure run by the administration and the faculty; a set of extracurricular activities sponsored, or approved of, by the administration (programs such as literary societies, religious and social clubs, and the like); and, finally, the network of student interactions. This third area was very diverse and included groups of dormitory residences, fraternity brothers and sorority sisters, and other groups that coalesced more or less informally. The key variable in these groups, Fass indicates, was that they were "within the control of the youth themselves." There were college rules of all sorts governing youthful behavior, but the norms for student behavior in these informal relationships were set by the young people themselves.[40]

Over the course of the two decades between the wars, the makeup of student bodies changed slightly. In 1920 women comprised 47.3 percent of all college students. By 1930 their percentage had fallen to 43.7, and a decade later to 40.2. This decline continued, not reversing itself until 1950 and not reaching the 1920 level again until 1980. From 1920 to 1980, the enrollment of women college students increased in every decade, although not as rapidly as the numbers of men students. The percentage of young women between the ages of 18 and 21 who went to college during the interwar period also climbed, rising from 7.6 in 1920 to 12.2 in 1940.[41]

Most women college students attended large, predominantly white, coeducational institutions, but in the 1920s and afterward, there were an increasing number of women's colleges from which to choose. The increase was especially notable among Catholic women's colleges; there were 14 in 1915 and 37 in 1925. Many students worked or contributed to their own educational costs. Of women students, from 32 to 40 percent held jobs in order to help pay their own costs at coeducational institutions, whereas at women's colleges, the percentage was only about 15. About half the men in college worked.[42]

When the depression threatened to reduce student enrollments in colleges and universities, a New Deal program came to the rescue. The National Youth Administration spent more than $93 million to give aid to about one in eight college students from 1935 to 1943. Although the amount of aid was small in many cases, it allowed many young people to remain in school.[43]

Conclusion

The expansion of schools and colleges, the rise in enrollments, and the broadening of curricula and options pointed to the increasing significance of schools and schooling in American life during the interwar period. This also meant that children and young people were more likely to have a common experience than ever before in American history. That this expansion was also accompanied by a growth in uniformity indicates that schools, like other agencies of socialization and acculturation in American life, greatly contributed to the development of mass culture and mass society. Although schools claimed to meet the needs of individual children, the experts they hired used standardized tests to determine what every child's needs were. Schools and colleges became increasingly bureaucratized and professionalized and as a result became less and less susceptible to the influences of the communities they served or the children they shaped. Communities sometimes resisted the directions the schools took, but for the most part, the schools were very popular with their constituents, and as a result, their expertise was seldom questioned. In colleges and high schools, young people were able to exercise some control over their lives through the peer societies they managed. Adults tried through activities they sponsored to control youthful leisure, but from 1920 on, more and more control passed from adults to youth, even as educational institutions became more centralized and thereby less susceptible to community or customer influence of any kind. As a result, although children and youth may have had some space they could call their own, much of their time was spent in highly regimented places where conformity, rather than creativity, was the norm.

4

The Federal Children's Bureau

The quintessential progressive federal agency was the Federal Children's Bureau. Created in 1912 as an outgrowth of the 1909 White House Conference on Children and the national anti–child labor movement, the bureau was limited in scope and funds and staffed predominantly with a new class of single professional women. The bureau's primary mission was to study problems relating to children and to make recommendations. Starting essentially from scratch, the first chief, Julia Lathrop, former Hull House resident and close personal friend of Jane Addams, must have been very nearly overwhelmed.[1]

The idea for the Children's Bureau had come from Lillian Wald and Florence Kelley, both of whom had had considerable experience with social causes and settlement house work by the early twentieth century. They had been outraged that the federal government would appropriate funds for the eradication of the boll weevil while denying any assistance to children—especially given the very high infant death rate in the United States at that time. Not all states registered births or kept vital statistics, but in those that did, the infant mortality rate in 1910 was 124 out of 1,000, or more than 10 times the late-twentieth-century rate. The bill to create the bureau was first introduced in 1906, and from year to year after that, support mounted across the country until the bureau was finally established in 1912.[2]

The Children's Bureau was housed in the Department of Labor and was thought of as a fact-finding agency. From the beginning, Lathrop sought professional women to staff the bureau. Historian Robyn Muncy believes that Lathrop wanted staffers who were both professionals and advocates. The early staffers tended to be white, middle-class, Midwestern in origin, and single, and many, such as Emma Lundberg and Katharine Lenroot, had worked in settlement houses.[3] The original staff numbered 15 and included Mary Mills West, a widow and mother and the author of the bureau's first enormously popular pamphlet, *Infant Care.* This pamphlet and its companion, *Prenatal Care,* helped to establish the reputation of the Children's Bureau as the principal source for up-to-date information on babies and children. Very early in the life of the bureau, the staff began a campaign to create a national system of birth registration so that accurate statistics on infant mortality could be gathered. To undertake this project, staffers relied on their network of supporters in women's clubs and other women's organizations.[4] As historian Robyn Muncy puts it, "by allying itself with female voluntary organizations, the Children's Bureau was marking child welfare as the preserve of female policy makers."[5]

The women who staffed the Children's Bureau saw themselves as both professionals and advocates. They believed that social action required the development of reliable information first and that once that information was properly understood, appropriate actions would follow. Early in its life, the bureau also published pamphlets on milk and midwifery. From 1916 to 1918, the bureau also controlled the enforcement of the Federal Child Labor Law until it was declared unconstitutional. Grace Abbott, who would be the bureau chief during the twenties and for part of the thirties, headed this operation until the Supreme Court declared the child labor law unconstitutional in the case of *Hammer v. Dagenhart* in 1918.[6]

Many of the staffers at the Children's Bureau had been trained at the Chicago School of Civics (of the University of Chicago—it became the School of Social Service Administration in 1924) by Grace Abbott's sister Edith and Sophnisba Breckinridge. This connection, along with strong ties to Hull House, meant that the Children's Bureau had a distinctly "Chicago" flavor in its early days. This was significant because the dominant trend in social work in the 1920s was oriented toward psychiatry rather than social science. The School of Social Service Administration was strong on the use of statistics, for example, as a necessary background to the development of social policy.[7] Not surprisingly, one of the first projects the bureau undertook was a study of infant mortality in Johnstown, Pennsylvania. The bureau regarded infant mortality as more of an economic and social problem than a racial problem. According to historian Molly Ladd-Taylor, "the Children's Bureau investigators found a striking correlation between infant mortality and poverty. A child whose father earned under $521 a year was almost twice as likely to die as one whose father earned over $1,200, and infant deaths increased by 40 percent when homes did not have running water." The investigators also found that poor nutrition and the lack of prenatal care were primary factors in causing infant deaths. In particular, the bureau strongly recommended breast feeding.[8]

In 1919 the bureau organized and sponsored the second White House Conference on Children—exactly 10 years after the first. This one focused on child welfare and called for the universal availability of adequate health care.

The bureau also recommended a form of pension that would allow mothers to remain home while nursing. One reason for these recommendations was that World War I had revealed the sorry physical and mental state of American draftees—one-third of the men in the first draft had been rejected because of physiological inadequacies. During the war, the Children's Bureau had helped to develop a national network of volunteer women to promote child health. As part of this national campaign, the bureau designated 1918 as the "Children's Year." [9]

What followed from these efforts was a groundbreaking piece of legislation—the Sheppard-Towner Act, a plan for federal matching grants to states in support of maternal and child health. The plan had essentially been drafted by Julia Lathrop and the Federal Children's Bureau. The provisions of the act were something less than Lathrop had hoped for, but the law itself set a precedent for the involvement of the federal government in health care. The act provided for instruction in, and information about, nutrition and hygiene and the establishment of prenatal clinics for pregnant women, child health clinics, and visiting nurses. In essence, it was an information-based preventative health care program. It was thus not based on a medical model of the treatment of disease and did not provide funds for the use of physicians. The law passed easily, historians believe, because politicians did not know what newly enfranchised women might do and because there had been strong support for the measure from a wide variety of women's groups. Another factor was the emergence of what Molly Ladd-Taylor calls a "maternalist" ideology and movement, which supported the idea of mothers' pensions as well as access to health care for women and children. [10]

All but three states (Massachusetts, Connecticut, and Illinois) passed enabling legislation that allowed the programs under the Sheppard-Towner act to begin. States held health conferences, distributed Children's Bureau pamphlets, began programs of birth registration, encouraged the use of silver nitrate to prevent infant blindness, provided training for midwives, and set up health clinics for mothers and babies. Although the program promoted employment for some women, especially nurses, it also depended heavily on volunteers, most of whom were women, to spread the word about the new programs. In rural states, where the population was scattered, nurses used home visits to distribute information and promote maternal and child health. [11]

Nurses, who were almost always white and well educated, encountered a number of obstacles to their work. Some women were too embarrassed to allow examinations or even discussions pertaining to childbirth. Others were suspicious of the scientific information the nurses dispensed. Racial and ethnic differences compounded the nurses' difficulties. These problems were especially acute on Indian reservations and among African-Americans. Cultural differences and mutual mistrust meant that in some cases the Sheppard-

Towner program was limited to white mothers and their children. Sometimes the problems with peoples of color stemmed from the decentralized way the programs were administered—with the result that services were not as readily available to Native Americans and African-Americans.[12]

Opposition to the Sheppard-Towner Act had been present even as it was passed, but when the bill for extending it came up in 1926, there was obdurate and organized opposition to renewal in the Senate, and supporters had to accept a compromise that would shut down Sheppard-Towner in 1929. Children's Bureau staffers, including Grace Abbott, believed that they could rally enough support from the ranks of women who had lobbied for the passage of the bill in the first place to continue the program. Fourteen separate bills to do just that were introduced, but all failed. Once it was known that women would not vote as a bloc, politicians realized that they need no longer fear reprisals at the polls. The newly enfranchised women were systematically excluded from the inner circles of political discourse, so that their ability to influence legislation was minimal.

Sheppard-Towner was in essence a piece of "progressive" legislation—in many respects, it was out of touch with the political temper of the times. By 1929 most Americans probably agreed that child health was a family, not a state, responsibility. Intense lobbying by the American Medical Association contributed to the act's defeat, and the failure of Sheppard-Towner to win the support of this powerful lobby probably doomed any hope of permanence for the program from the start.

This view prevailed even though Sheppard-Towner, if judged by its announced purposes, was a success. Infant mortality declined from 76 to 69 per 1,000 live births in the period when the program was in effect. Maternal mortality declined, too, from 67 to 64 per 10,000 live births. The program registered a slight improvement in the infant mortality rates for African-Americans as well, even though many African-Americans were beyond the reach of the program or too poor to take advantage of all it had to offer.[13]

During the 1920s, the Children's Bureau also supported the campaign for a federal child labor amendment, but this effort never coalesced into a movement strong enough to move seriously for a constitutional amendment. Although bureau staffers still felt strongly that some sort of national statement about the evils of child labor needed to be made, they could take comfort from the fact that child labor itself was declining. Most states had compulsory school attendance laws by the 1920s, and they, rather than child labor laws, were effective in reducing child labor. Even more effective, though, were technological changes that reduced the demand for child labor, especially in southern cotton mills.[14]

The 1920s was also a time of increasing awareness of the prestige of science on the part of the Children's Bureau. Mary Mills West's practical advice gave way to that of a pediatrician, because, she was told, her views were insufficiently scientific. Science was all the rage, and civic and philanthropic leaders rushed to apply it to social problems, especially those pertaining to children. Like the reformers before them, the social leaders of the 1920s believed that they could remedy social ills and shape the future if they could address the problems of children in the present.[15]

In some respects, the decision to replace Mrs. West was unfortunate, because her version of *Infant Care* certainly commanded strong popular support. Letters to the bureau attest to the pamphlet's importance and tell of tattered copies being passed from household to household. A distinguishing feature of West's *Infant Care* is that it recognized the situation most mothers were in and advised accordingly. A great many mothers wrote to the bureau— sometimes over 100,000 in a year—and their letters indicated that women of all sorts, including the very poor for whom the pamphlets were intended, looked upon the bureau as a friend and appropriate source of information. According to historian Nancy Pottishman Weiss, the staffers of the bureau did more than simply reply to the letters: "Acting as a cluster of individuals rather than as a federal agency, bureau members provided their correspondents with help in the way of layettes, medical care for lying-in, and donations of money."[16]

When the spell of science cost Mrs. West her job, the notion that some concern for mothers should be included in the pamphlet also went out. Behaviorism—particularly as described by John B. Watson—was the dominant paradigm in child-rearing advice, and Watson himself was opposed to mothers and motherhood as being too sentimental. Mothers were old-fashioned and unscientific and thus impediments to the new proper rearing of children. At any rate, concerns for mothers were out—in the pamphlet perhaps, but not necessarily in the minds of the staffers.[17]

Meanwhile, mothers continued to write to the Children's Bureau in great numbers. One mother, having taken her one-year-old to see a doctor, wondered about the doctor's advice not to feed the child vegetables. The mother had followed the advice in *Infant Care*, and the baby was "in excellent health." Another mother wrote to ask why her doctor was recommending a "formula" for her infant, then aged 12 weeks. "I do not understand why I cannot nurse him as at first," she wrote. She asked the doctor a second time, and he suggested weaning. The Children's Bureau wrote back with a number of helpful suggestions and strongly encouraged her to continue breast-feeding. A Michigan mother wondered why she seemed not to have enough milk on laundry day. A bureau staffer wrote in reply: "Would it be possible for you to divide your washing over several days, doing a little at a time so that you would not become so completely worn out?"[18]

Other mothers worried about the "bad habits" their babies and children had. This concern is not surprising because the dominant mode of child rearing in the 1920s was the development of good habits in children and the elim-

ination of the bad. Thus, in a sense, child rearing was a matter of habit training, or an essential kind of behaviorism. A mother from Washington, D.C.,
worried because her child cried whenever she went out and wondered if it
were "too late to train him not to cry after me." A bureau staffer replied that
"it is never too late to begin training and disciplining a child." When a New
Jersey mother wrote about her baby daughter's excessive masturbation, the
staffer replied by suggesting some toys to distract the baby and counseled the
mother not to be "too concerned," as "she is very likely to outgrow it." For
thumb sucking, staffers recommended devices such as cardboard cuffs that
would prevent infants from bringing their thumbs to their mouths.[19]

Other mothers who wrote were concerned about their babies' illnesses,
and bureau staffers wrote back, consistently suggesting that the mothers consult physicians. Sometimes mothers wrote about the deaths of their babies. In
1917 Mrs. W. D. of Brooklyn wrote:

> A year ago last Mr. I gave birth to a beautiful fat boy and it lived but 3 days. The
> Drs. claimed the baby had a leaking heart; he died in convulsions. I would like to
> know if the injection the *woman* [sic] gave him of soap and water threw him in
> these convulsions as he just moaned like a pigeon & his whole body shook after
> that & at night he was dead. This was the first time I became pregnant in 4 yrs.
> and you can imagine how glad & happy I was, only instead of having him at my
> breast, the third day they brought him to the door in his little casket.

Three months later, she was pregnant again. She gave birth to another boy,
who lived a little more than a year before he, too, died. "I am stout and as a
rule healthy," she continued, but "I can't understand why my babies should
have weak hearts." Mrs. West urged the mother to "go to the best doctor you
can find" so that he could "study your case and try to help you."

A grieving mother from Illinois told a similar story. Her baby boy died
after four months. "i could not nurse my baby," she confessed, "and he just
faded away, never gaining, or rather losing weight on all the many foods
which the different doctors tried." Staffers wrote back to grieving mothers,
expressing sympathy and in some cases reassuring mothers that they had not
through some inadvertent action caused the death of their babies.[20]

Another difficulty many of the mothers who wrote to the Children's Bureau
faced was their own poverty; they could not afford the measures the bureau
pamphlets recommended. Others describe the realities of living with multiple
small children and the many burdens of housework. One expectant mother was
particularly distressed because her husband had been injured and she was without funds and "only camping and living in a shack and tent." In this case, bureau
staffers contacted the Child Health Department of California, which in turn
arranged for a local women's club to provide assistance. Other mothers wrote
complaining about their poverty and in the process said that if the country was
serious about helping children, it needed to help mothers as well:

God help the poor mothers of today. The cry is Save the babies, but what about the mothers who produce these babies? Now dear sirs, No hard feeling for what I have written. But would it not be better to enact a law that, when a man marries a woman and she bears his children for him, that he be compelled to provide for the babies he caused to be brought into the world. . . . And if possible start an association to protect mothers who are to give birth and after that help them to do for their babies. The Soldier receives his pension. What do mothers receive? Abuse, torture, slurs, that is the best they receive. Men in long service receive their pension. Mothers deserving receiv[e] nothing.[21]

As it happened, the idea of mothers' pensions was already being talked about in several circles, including the Children's Bureau.

The idea behind mothers' pensions was that mothers could be paid small sums so that their children would not have to go to institutions. The first state to pass such a law was Illinois in 1911. Many different progressive reform groups endorsed the idea, as it seemed to promise not only to reduce the cost of caring for dependent children but also to be better for the children because they could remain in their own home. By 1919, 41 states had adopted mothers' pension laws. The payments, which were very small, went only to deserving women who were either widows or who had been deserted. The laws were permissive, rather than mandatory, and many local jurisdictions simply ignored them. Also, because only "fit" mothers were eligible for the money, agents of the local governments pried into the private lives of poor women to make sure they met the moral requirements for aid.

Because there was never enough money to fund the program adequately, aid was dispensed according to a set of preferences that put widows of English descent at the top and abandoned or unwed mothers at the bottom (few of them ever got aid). Immigrant women and African-American women received aid less often than women of Anglo-Saxon descent. As a consequence, most single mothers were forced to seek work in order to support their children. Social workers did not necessarily condemn this, as the mothers frequently had no choice. A Children's Bureau study completed in 1923 found that over half the mothers in the study worked for wages. Of that number, about half worked outside the home, and the remainder brought work into their homes.[22]

By the 1920s, the consensus that had supported the idea of mothers' pensions at the beginning of the century had dissolved. The idea had quickly won favor; women's lobbying groups had moved on to other issues such as child labor; and women's clubs seemed not to have been concerned about the administration of the pensions. One reason was that the aid was no longer being considered a pension but rather was a part of the rise of social casework and the application of proper remedies to individual situations. More fundamentally, according to Molly Ladd-Taylor, the system heightened class differences. "Although the rhetoric of mothers' pension supporters stressed the common bonds of motherhood, the welfare system increased the power some women had to take away the livelihood—and the children—of others, and it highlighted the divisions between them."[23]

In August 1921, Grace Abbott succeeded Julia Lathrop as chief of the Children's Bureau. Under her leadership, the bureau continued its study of maternal and infant mortality. In 1922 the bureau issued *The Nutrition and Care of Children in a Mountain County of Kentucky,* and in 1933, *Maternal Deaths: Brief Report of a Study Made in Fifteen States.* Other topics under study included the prevention of rickets, services for crippled children, child dependency, foster care, children born out of wedlock, adoption, recreation, mental defectives, juvenile and family courts, and various other aspects of child welfare. The bureau, of course, also monitored the Sheppard-Towner Act provisions and lobbied on behalf of a federal anti–child labor amendment. In addition, in the last part of the decade, the bureau was busy preparing for the 1930 White House conference on children.[24]

The study of rickets (a disease caused by the deficiency of vitamin D) began in 1924 and was directed by Dr. Martha Eliot, a pediatrician on the bureau staff in Hartford, Connecticut. Results of the study showed that rickets was easily prevented or treated if infants received sufficient exposure to sunlight or a sufficient dose of cod-liver oil.[25]

When the bureau looked at maternal mortality, it found that lack of prenatal care was a dominant factor—over half the mothers in the study had had no prenatal care. Some deaths were due to sepsis or infection contracted during delivery. Some mothers died as a result of botched abortions. Still others died from complications of pregnancy, such as toxemia. The study recommended that prenatal care be extended to all mothers. This meant that doctors should take the lead in informing the public of the importance of prenatal care (something already clearly demonstrated by Sheppard-Towner) and that doctors should also provide leadership in organizing "the available resources of their communities [so] that every mother can receive adequate medical care." The report also recommended that the general public be told that most maternal deaths were due to controllable causes and that "the community has a definite responsibility to provide adequate medical care and nursing facilities for the care of women during pregnancy, labor, and the postpartum period."[26]

In 1924 the bureau began a study of the adequacy of child welfare services in the state of Georgia, followed by a similar study of services in Minnesota, North Dakota, South Dakota, North Carolina, Pennsylvania, and New York. These studies led to a conference sponsored by the bureau and held in Washington, D.C., in 1929. The conference concluded that state programs for child welfare should strive to do more than simply supervise institutions. This would place a greater emphasis on social casework and on preserving the family of the child at risk. Unfortunately, the Great Depression intervened before this grand vision could be implemented.[27]

The bureau also lent its prestige to the growing number of juvenile courts in the country by publishing *Standards for Juvenile Courts,* a set of benchmarks by which local courts could measure their practices. In 1928 the bureau began to encourage the courts to adapt uniform standards for the reporting of their cases. In 1930 the bureau published a study on the causes of delinquency, and in 1932 Congress passed a bill allowing juvenile federal offenders to be tried in local juvenile courts.[28]

Throughout the 1920s, the bureau wrestled with the problem of mental retardation or mental deficiency. The problem had many dimensions. Some parents wrote to the bureau looking for institutions or programs, whereas others sought individual help. For example, in May 1930, a mother from Glenside, Pennsylvania, wrote about her son:

> After hearing your interesting talk over the radio this evening I hope I am not expecting too much in asking your advice in this matter.
>
> My little boy is 9 years 5 months old. He is a backward child but not an impossible one. When he was 7 years old, I thought I'd enter him in school but the lady psychiatrist, or whatever her title is insisted he was not for public education. After considerable fussing I got them to try him out. They promoted him along from 1st to 2nd and his teachers were nice about him. He was troublesome when it came to desk work but when he was taking part in the study he was allright. . . . when fall came of this year I received notice that a test by the psychiatrist from Harrisburg stated he should have private tutoring. My dear Miss Abbott would we not do all that if we could afford it? They were heartless in their remarks. Said I wouldn't raise him, the state don't bother about an individual and if Philadelphia had such good special classes they suggested I move back there. . . .
>
> Miss Abbott, Samuel reads, writes, spells, adds and subtracts a little. Now could he do this even on a small scale, had I not helped him? Should not this Weldon-Glenside school provide a special class?. . . . His doctor who treated him from 7 months to 5 years thinks he most certainly is entitled to public education. . . .
>
> Now tell me Miss Abbott am I taking the wrong attitude in fighting this school. Would you try and get him into Phila and pay the extra city tax. (I'm out of the city limits) Maybe they would not be nice to him beings I fought them. . . . Please tell me what you think best.

Abbott wrote back sympathetically, noting, "I realize that under the circumstances you are finding the problem of school training for your boy extremely difficult." Abbott recommended that the mother place her son in the special classes of the Philadelphia schools, noting that "very few small places provide such classes, and if they do the classes are not of the same quality as you will find in a large city."[29]

Sam did find a place in a program that was designed to meet his needs, but he had to go back into the city instead of staying in the closer country school. During the twenties, special programs for mentally handicapped children were by no means universal, but the Children's Bureau made this area one of its major emphases. In September 1924, for example, the bureau received a letter from Pathfinders of America, who styled themselves "human engineers" and claimed that they were "for every nationality, Color, Tongue, and Creed." Pathfinders was trying to drum up support for their activities in the field of mental hygiene, and they also asked for "any circulars or material that will benefit us." They had written to the Children's Bureau, "realizing their intense interest in mental hygiene." A similar letter came from the Public Charities Association of Pennsylvania, inquiring about "habit clinics" and "child guidance clinics." Abbott wrote back indicating that the bureau was preparing a publication on habit training.[30] In August 1924, Dr. V. V. Anderson wrote to Emma Lundberg at the bureau to indicate that he was planning to leave the National Committee for Mental Hygiene and "open a private hospital-school for the study, treatment and training of problem children, with special reference to those suffering from conduct disorders,—the so-called behavior field of childhood." Anderson had a thorough, well-ordered program in mind:

> It will be my aim to bring to bear on these problems every facility that medicine, psychiatry, educational psychology, and a model controlled environment can offer. All of the advantages of physical training, shop work, intensive academic instruction, approved recreational facilities, farm life, as well as modern psychiatric treatment will be offered.

Lundberg wrote back, "delighted to hear you have opened a private hospital for problem children." She added: "From our correspondence with people who are seeking just this type of care for children I know that you are undertaking a most important piece of work. I am glad to know of it as we recently have inquiries." But Lundberg worried about the cost, especially for "the less well-to-do," because many of the inquiries came from poor people. "Perhaps in working out your venture you will also be contributing ideas that will lead to the establishment of similar hospital schools that may be within the reach of families who cannot afford to pay a large amount." In October 1924, Anderson wrote again to announce that he had retired from the National Committee for Mental Hygiene and that he was now prepared to take children privately at the rate of $125 per month. He said nothing about schools for troubled children from poorer families. This exchange shows that the bureau frequently received inquiries about mentally handicapped or troubled children and served as a kind of clearinghouse in this newly developing field. One response the bureau gave to inquires about children who had mental deficiency was to suggest readings such as Arnold Gesell's *The Retarded Child: How to Help Him*.[31]

Sometimes inquiries came from farther away. In 1929 William McCloy, representing the Central Council of Social Agencies in Winnipeg, Manitoba, wrote seeking assistance as his committee prepared to make recommendations to the Provincial Government. He was especially concerned about people who had severe retardation:

> There seems to be no discussion in regard to the idiot and imbecile class, for whom institutional care is absolutely necessary. In regard to morons and low grade morons, different opinions are held amongst us, some favoring full institutional care, and others a period of training in an institution, followed by employment at whatever task the people are fitted to perform. Again in the higher types it is questioned if there should be institutional care at all, even for a period, since some deem the children's own homes or foster homes, under supervision, as the best place for training and development. In addition, of course to special classes in school, etc.

McCloy's letter is revealing in that it shows how the public generally classified children with mental deficiencies, and it shows a recognition of public responsibilities for mentally handicapped children.[32]

The defeat of the Sheppard-Towner Act and the coming of the Great Depression both had major impacts on the Children's Bureau. The loss of Sheppard-Towner deprived the bureau of the mission of directly supervising services. And the depression meant the bureau would be less able to be an advocate for new approaches to issues such as infant mortality rates and mentally handicapped children. But the bureau was able to be a part of the New Deal and played a significant part in the passage of the Social Security Act.

In 1934 Katharine Lenroot succeeded Grace Abbott as bureau chief. Lenroot had been with the bureau since 1915. When Lenroot came on board, her boss, Frances Perkins (the secretary of labor), sat on the Committee on Economic Security, which also included the secretary of agriculture and the chief administrator of the Federal Emergency Relief Agency. Roosevelt had established the committee to study the best approach to a system of old-age pensions and to forestall congressional action in the area. Because of the Children's Bureau's longtime support of mothers' pensions and because of concern for children, who, it was clear, had suffered a great deal during the depression, the bureau was in a key position to influence any legislation pertaining to economic security.

Three women, Abbott, Lenroot, and Dr. Martha Eliot, were asked by Secretary Perkins to make recommendations about children's programs that might be included in the legislation. They recommended four programs: an expanded, federally funded program of mothers' pensions, now called Aid to Dependent Children; expanded services for homeless, neglected, and dependent children; maternal and child health programs (essentially the same as Sheppard-Towner); and special services for crippled children. During the depression, these programs were not controversial—there were many other far more extreme proposals to worry about, and so the programs for children were included in the Social Security Act of 1935. Unlike the Sheppard-

Towner programs, the new programs under Social Security were essentially medical in orientation (except for ADC) and were designed for indigent families, rather than for everyone.[33]

It now fell to the bureau to administer these new programs. All 48 states cooperated with the bureau on the maternal and child health programs. The idea was to provide money to state health departments so that they could hire physicians, nurses, dentists, and other professionals to provide health care in rural areas.[34] The program focused on the prevention of infant and maternal deaths and on the training of health care professionals. Later in the decade, special demonstration projects for the improvement of maternal and infant health became a major focus. The program provided very little direct health care.[35]

By 1937, 42 states had joined the crippled children's program, and by the next year, all but one state had joined. Most made this program a part of their state health departments. In this program, a considerable effort to provide services was central. States went to considerable lengths to find crippled children and bring them in for services. Some funds also went for the training of personnel.[36]

Children's Bureau staffers had long been active in the study and promotion of welfare services for children. Their 1919 publication *Standards of Child Welfare* was just the beginning of the bureau's concern in this area, but in the 1930s, with funding provided through the Social Security Act, the bureau's activities expanded. Each state developed its own plan for services and worked in cooperation with the bureau, which now functioned in its familiar clearinghouse role. For example, one major decision was to favor programs for training staff in various state welfare programs rather than to provide money for foster care. In effect, the bureau voted for more social casework rather than for the direct provision of services.[37]

The bureau continued to receive many letters, some having been handed over from the White House—many Americans believed that President Roosevelt would be personally interested in their problems and so wrote directly to him. Others wrote directly to the bureau and asked for specific sorts of help. In May 1933, the secretary of the Rotary Club in Ashland, Wisconsin, wrote asking for help for their committee on boys' work. Bureau staffer Agnes Hanna wrote back, enclosing a copy of the bureau publication *Facts about Juvenile Delinquency* and several other items and referring the Rotarians to *Parents' Magazine*. Hanna added in conclusion, "if you have not already done so, we would suggest that you get in touch with various organization engaged particularly to work for boys, such as the Boy Scouts, the Boy Rangers, or Pioneer Youth of Arizona."[38]

Sometimes aspiring child trainers wrote to solicit the bureau's reaction to their ideas. One F. A. Bean sent the bureau a letter in March 1933. Dr. Ella Oppenheimer, a bureau staffer and physician, wrote back to say that she would look it over. Persistent with his ideas, Bean wrote back in May to ask why he had heard nothing. Oppenheimer finally responded on May 20, raising serious objections to Bean's scheme of using financial rewards as a way of training children in proper manners and behavior. "It seems to be fundamentally unsound," Oppenheimer wrote, "to put the matter of attending to the routine matters of life such as getting up on time, getting to school on time, etc., in terms of earning and for that matter, saving money." Oppenheimer also criticized Bean for the severity of some of his proposed punishments and added that "the positive value of this system could probably be obtained equally well, given the same family make up and emotional balance, without such a formal outline as set up."[39]

Letters from troubled parents seeking help for their children also poured in. In January 1934, having heard a radio talk by Dr. Oppenheimer, a mother wrote asking what she might do with a daughter who had school problems and seemed to have developed bad personal habits that were disrupting her classes. Oppenheimer referred her to Dr. Marion Kenworthy, the medical director of the New York School of Social Work, and also suggested that she look into the possibility of special classes in her school system. Another mother wrote in great detail to Oppenheimer in July 1935, worried about her 12-year-old daughter, who seemed to have an inferiority complex. Obviously interested in the case, even though her first recommendation was to "consult someone who is experienced in helping children and parents work out their problems," Oppenheimer continued for another two single-spaced pages with various suggestions. Thus the bureau, in addition to its own programs, continued to be a kind of national referral and problem-solving agency where children were concerned. In this respect, certainly, Americans felt closer to their federal government than they ever had before.[40]

The bureau no doubt hoped that its radio programs and the continuing publication program would help to educate the public and thereby reduce the number of letters coming in. In some respects, the opposite was true. Once people learned about the existence of the bureau, they seemed eager for more information. And as the letters kept coming, so the bureau also saw its work expand during the 1930s. It administered the programs established under Social Security and contributed to the passage of the Fair Labor Standards Act, the first permanent federal anti–child labor law. Toward the end of the decade, the bureau was occupied in planning the 1940 White House Conference on Children in a Democracy, the title itself showing where the fears of the nation were as World War II broke out in Europe.

The Children's Bureau was an unusual federal agency because it developed and maintained a close relationship with the American people. Long before Americans began writing President Roosevelt, American mothers wrote to the bureau for advice and help with their children. In the early days, bureau staffers sometimes even dipped into their own resources to provide help. Throughout the two decades between the wars, this agency provided both a federal presence in many homes and a human response to pressing problems. To be sure, the bureau's public stance and most of its responses reflected the biases and presumptions of its predominantly middle-class white female staff, and it sought to develop national standards for the care of children, believing that it had a clear mandate to do so. Yet its work certainly made a difference. Sheppard-Towner reduced infant mortality rates, and bureau efforts fostered better juvenile courts and better programs for the mentally handicapped. The bureau's contribution to Social Security affected generations of children born long after the period. It is hard not to argue that children were better off because of the bureau's work.

5

Child Science, Guidance Clinics, and the Rise of Experts: The Reconstruction of Childhood in the United States

The modern era in the history of childhood in the United States began when children became the objects of study of people who called themselves scientists, who regarded their methods as scientific and what they were doing as producing science. The rise of these "experts" in child science ushered in a new era in the way American society regarded its children and thereby profoundly altered the contexts in which American society regarded children. This change is best understood in terms of contrasts. Before child science had legitimated the idea of age-graded elementary education, before it had classified students based on the construction of the concept of intelligence quotient, and before psychologists had been enlisted as the appropriate arbiters of developmental truth in American society, childhood was a much softer social institution. Children attended school haphazardly and in accordance with other rhythms in their lives. Children moved in and out of the paid workforce in accordance with the waxing and waning of family fortunes. Children left home and entered the adult world in a long and gradual process, confident that their family of origin could function as a safety net if need be. They worked for a time away from home, came back when the work ran out, and left again to seek their fortunes. The basic metaphor for the preparation for adulthood was apprenticeship.[1]

The modern age was characterized by a different process. School was the dominant metaphor; it was the necessary gate through which all successful adults would pass. It was the means by which children learned the central values of their conformist, capitalist, white male culture, and it was beyond question an important social institution because scientists and politicians alike agreed on its universal necessity.

This chapter will discuss public reactions to the rise of child science and the popularization of its tenets through the national media in the 1920s and 1930s. The development of child science was a triumph of science over social reform; that is, studying normal children became more important than ameliorating the lives of "problem" children. In the evolution of child science, the key roles were played by large foundations and their agents, among whom the most notable was Lawrence K. Frank, who served both the Laura Spelman Rockefeller Memorial and the General Education Board of the Rockefeller Foundation. Two principal designs were prominent in the early 1920s. The first, sponsored by the Laura Spelman Rockefeller Memorial, at first emphasized the development of a science of the normal child. The second, sponsored by the Commonwealth Fund, attacked the problem of juvenile delinquency with the forces of psychiatry and psychoanalysis. Both claimed the mantle of science and thus related directly to the nation's passion for scientific solutions to social problems.

A number of factors had come together to allow child science to expand so rapidly in the 1920s and 1930s. Such rapid growth could not have happened without the infusion of large (at least by academic standards of the period) sums of money; it could not have happened without a strong social interest in children—an interest that had survived the Great War—even though many concerns of the Progressive Era had not. The horrors of the war made people want to forget it and build a better future, and the woeful physical and mental conditions of American draftees inspired American reformers to address the deficiencies of childhood. The expansion of child science also could not have happened without the support of key figures such as Robert S. Woodworth of the Columbia University Psychology Department. Woodworth supported the idea of child science and became the chair of the National Research Council's Division of Anthropology and Psychology in 1924. Woodworth and Bird T. Baldwin of the Iowa Child Welfare Research Station changed the name of the Child Welfare Committee, which Baldwin had chaired, to the Child Development Committee, thus rescuing child science at the national level from its social welfare associations.[2] Child science also could not have flourished without the availability of a number of highly trained professionals who were not otherwise employed. The fact that a number of women fit this description meant, ironically, that child science was the beneficiary of profound sexism in the behavioral sciences because women rarely found places in the "regular" academic departments.[3]

Although there had been some academic interest in child study and child psychology before the end of World War I—notably the work of G. Stanley Hall—the real explosion came after the war. In some cases, entirely new programs, such as the Child Development Institute at Teacher's College of Columbia University, were created, whereas in others, existing programs, such as the one at the Merrill Palmer School in Detroit, were modified or expanded. Sometimes the new child science institutes and research stations were affiliated with the psychology department, as was the case at Berkeley, and sometimes they were entirely separate, as seemed to be the case at Minnesota and Iowa. But these programs were unified by a central purpose: the creation of a science of the normal child.[4]

American physicians and psychologists were shocked at the poor physical and psychological condition of the draftees during World War I. Far too many young men were either poorly fed or suffering from serious physical ailments. Still more shocking was the poor educational background of many of the draftees. Although some experts, including many psychologists, argued that the IQ tests given during World War I showed that many Americans—especially the recent immigrants—were mentally deficient, others, particularly school officials, believed that the poor showing of the draftees reflected an inadequate educational background. The solutions to these problems were a national focus on improving health care for children, which would lead to increased education about child health care and parent education; a renewed interest in the expansion of educational opportunities, which would have the important by-product of stemming child labor, a major threat to the well-being of American youth; and the creation of a body of expertise about children, which could be used to shape public policies pertaining to children and solve social problems involving children.

After the war, many Americans also believed that American youth were out of control. In the public mind, at least, the threat of juvenile delinquency preempted all other issues pertaining to children and youth. One agency willing to address this concern was the Commonwealth Fund, which had been established in 1918 by Anna Harkness, the widow of Stephen Harkness, who had made his money by investing in John D. Rockefeller's Standard Oil Company. The charter of the fund was vague: it was "to do something for the benefit of mankind."[5] Historian Max Farrand of Yale, the fund's director, concluded in 1920 that juvenile delinquency was a social problem worthy of the fund's attention for two reasons: it was an issue that had aroused public interest, and so far no other foundation had put any money into it.

Much had already been done about delinquency. Juvenile courts had been created across the country, following the Illinois precedent of 1899, and many courts tried to make use of the services of various experts in their communities. Chicago pioneered in the establishment of a clinic that would bring the power of science to bear on the problem. The Juvenile Psychopathic Institute chose Julia Lathrop of Hull House as president and William A. Healy as director. Healy had a broad medical and psychiatric background and set to work in 1909 to try to find the scientific causes of delinquency, which he believed would enable him to make recommendations for its prevention. Despite prodigious efforts and a wealth of cases, Healy and his assistant, Augusta Bronner, were unable to pin down the causes or make specific recommendations. In a 1917 publication, Healy found that results of standard psychological tests and medical and family histories were inadequate to explain the causes of juvenile delinquency. In a few cases, Healy did find evidence of what he labeled "mental conflicts" and described as a "distinct inner urge towards mediocracy" that could be regarded as a causative factor. Because this pattern fit only 7 percent of more than a thousand cases, in the end, Healy could only call for more study, a call he repeated in a 1922 Children's Bureau pamphlet, *The Practical Value of the Scientific Study of Juvenile Delinquents.*[6] By that time, the Commonwealth Fund had decided to put its money into the scientific study of juvenile delinquency, but the people it had relied on as experts were really interested in mental hygiene, rather than delinquency.

As it turned out, the interest in juvenile delinquency waned rather quickly. According to historian Margo Horn, "delinquency proved of temporary relevance," because "psychiatrists' long-term interests lay not in delinquency but in treating milder mental health problems."[7] Even though in some senses Healy's work had been fruitless, the idea of promoting mental health was very attractive—in part because the idea had already attracted widespread public support through the activities of the National Committee for Mental Hygiene, established in 1909. At first, the committee had done research on conditions in asylums. During the war, it focused on some of the psychological problems associated with war, such as "shell shock," and after the war, it began a program of community education about the prevention of mental illness. To some, preventing mental illness and preventing juvenile delinquency were essentially the same activities. Both fell under the umbrella of "social psychiatry," and both were incorporated within the scope of a new professional organization. The American Orthopsychiatric Association, which was founded in 1924 and began the *Journal of Orthopsychiatry* in 1930, exemplified the national concern about mental hygiene.[8]

The board of the Commonwealth Fund supported a proposal from psychiatrist Bernard Glueck, who had been working with adult prisoners at Sing Sing Prison in New York, to establish a community mental health clinic that would work with predelinquent youth. In 1921 the fund also sponsored a conference of experts on the prevention of delinquency. The conference recognized the importance of social conditions, including poverty, in causing juvenile misbehavior, but they proposed better medical and psychological treatment of offenders and additional preventative measures rather than take on the difficult issues of race and class. Following the conference, the fund proposed a four-pronged attack on the problem of juvenile delinquency: (1) funding Glueck's clinic, which was associated with the New York School of

Social Work; (2) creating a division within the National Committee for Mental Hygiene to promote additional clinics; (3) establishing of a visiting teacher program to coordinate relations between home, school, and clinic; and (4) forming a Joint Committee on Methods of Preventing Delinquency, which would inform the public about the workings of the other parts of the program.[9] The Commonwealth Fund established seven demonstration clinics. Two, in St. Louis and Norfolk, were affiliated with courts; two, in Dallas and Los Angeles, were affiliated with hospitals. Freestanding clinics were established in Minneapolis, Philadelphia, and Cleveland.[10]

A typical clinic was that established in association with the Cleveland, Ohio, Children's Aid Society. In 1923 the clinic began operation under a psychiatrist as a mental study center for needy children. In 1924 the Commonwealth Fund provided money, and in 1926 a separate demonstration clinic was opened, becoming a full-fledged child guidance clinic in January 1927. It was reorganized, and its services were redefined as psychological and medical examinations for troubled children. Commonwealth Fund money lasted only two years, but the society continued the clinic as a part of its regular services. According to Lawrence Cole, who became the superintendent in 1928, for 10 years

> the Children's Aid Society has helped other social agencies find out why some children have trouble at home, in school, in boarding homes or institutions. Parents may seek institutional care for their children who disobey, run away, fight, or steal. These parents do not know why—they only know that they cannot put up with their trouble any longer. Agencies ask for the study of neglected and abused children to discover what damage may have been done to body or personality, and how best this damage can be corrected.[11]

Healy had not been able to find the causes of delinquency, and the psychiatrists who advised the Commonwealth Fund in its early days were willing to talk about delinquency but were ill prepared to do anything about preventing it. Consequently, the emerging mental hygiene movement among psychiatrists found other problems to address.

In the early days, however, clinic staffers did try, at least at Minnesota, to deal with delinquency. According to Willard Olson, who became a faculty member in Education at the University of Michigan:

> The general purpose of the guidance institute was the prevention of delinquency, and this eventually guided my doctoral dissertation, which had to do with problem tendencies in children. The clinic also stressed the multi-disciplinary approach; sociologists, psychologists, social workers, educators all working in concert to apply their fields and disciplines to the prevention of delinquency.[12]

By 1927 the clinics had shifted their focus to providing assistance to children who had emotional problems. A syndrome, that of the "problem child," was identified and became the focus of child guidance clinics. Problem children were the ones who refused to conform to the expectations of adults in the expanding public school systems. According to Horn, the issue was one of "maladjustment," which

> ranged from undesirable habits in younger children such as thumb-sucking, nail-biting, enuresis, masturbation, peculiar food fads, and night terrors, to personality traits such as sensitiveness, seclusiveness, apathy, excessive imagination, and fanciful lying. Also included was a category of undesirable behavior in older children, such as disobedience, teasing, bullying, temper tantrums, bragging, or showing off, defiance of authority, seeking bad companions, keeping late hours, and sexual activities.[13]

Rather deftly, the clinics had refocused their mission on problem children and in the process had restricted their concern to the ordinary problems of "normal children." Children with severe mental or physical problems were beyond the scope and mission of the child guidance clinics.

During this period, the number of clinics grew, and in 1927 the Commonwealth Fund changed its approach. It now supported the Division on Community Clinics of the National Committee for Mental Hygiene, which in turn provided assistance to newly formed clinics. Still, clinics multiplied, and by 1931 there were clinics in 23 cities and plans to create 10 more. Most clinics survived the depression, despite the fact that the Commonwealth Fund was no longer providing money for them. A few clinics, including those in New Orleans, Indianapolis, Detroit, Flint, and St. Louis, closed, as did the Institute for Child Guidance in New York City, the principal training site for child guidance professionals.[14]

By the end of the 1930s, the role and mission of the clinics had changed as well. In the beginning, they billed themselves as addressing a social problem, juvenile delinquency, by using preventative approaches. Clinics shifted their concern to problem children but retained a preventative approach during most of the 1920s, but by the 1930s, they had become medicalized and concentrated on treating individual emotional and psychological problems. For example, the purpose of the clinic at the East Bay Hospital in Berkeley, California, was "to provide services for the study and treatment of the emotionally-disturbed, socially-maladjusted, mentally-handicapped, or otherwise disordered child." According to an internal memorandum: "This would include about the same type of cases that we have seen during the past year," but cases would be selected on the basis of whether they "offered treatment possibilities," rather than on the basis of "the urgency of the problem."[15] As the clinics became medicalized, they found that the number of referrals initiated by parents increased. This was ironic, though, because the clinics had also begun to see the parents as having caused many of the children's problems.[16]

Psychiatric social workers in the child guidance clinics sought to enlist mothers in working on children's problems and at the same time began to blame mothers for the children's problems. That is, most of the social workers tended to see themselves as helping the child and correcting the mother. Mothers went along with this because they "were afforded emotional release through therapy designed specifically for them." At the same time, social workers "developed a clinical practice through their work with mothers." As a result of their clinical work with mothers and children, staffers came to the conclusion that many of the problems they saw might have been avoided through appropriate family life education.[17]

Even as the clinics themselves became medicalized, so some people clung to the early ideas about using the clinics to engineer major social change. In 1938 the commissioner of education called a conference to study "Organization for Clinical Adjustment of Behavior Problems in School Children." Most of those in attendance were school superintendents or supervisors of special education. A summary report of the conference concluded that

> The purpose of a clinical child guidance program is not limited to the adjustment of a comparatively small number of serious behavior problems; its influence should be preventive as well as remedial, and its service should be directly or indirectly to all the children in the school system. Psychological findings concerning the abilities and disabilities of children should help supervisors and teachers to make adequate curricular adjustments. Social work brings information concerning home and community environment and should assist in developing a close cooperation between home and school for all children. . . . Moreover, an effective child guidance program will be reflected in a more careful selection of teachers, with attention to desirable personality and emotional adjustment of the candidates as well as to their intellectual qualifications.[18]

There clearly was a sense, at least on the part of school administrators, that social purposes and preventative approaches were still desirable and that schools, aided by new expertise, were the best means of accomplishing those goals.[19]

While child guidance clinics were evolving, child science was also undergoing major changes. Just after World War I, the prestige of science, particularly human science, was very high in American society. As we have seen, psychiatrists were willing to take on the issue of juvenile delinquency through the child guidance clinics supported by the Commonwealth Fund. Thus they addressed the social and psychological pathology of youth using psychoanalytic approaches. Still to be addressed was the question of a science of "normal" children. Implicit in the response of social scientists to the issues of post–World War I America was the need for such a science as a basis for major social improvement. "In order to justify their appropriation of parental functions," historian Christopher Lasch wrote, the "helping professions" in their formative period—roughly from 1900 to 1930—appealed many times to the analogy of preventative medicine and public health. Educators, psychiatrists, social workers, and penologists saw themselves as doctors to a sick society, and they demanded the broadest possible delegation of medical authority in order to heal it.[20]

Another historian, Sonya Michel, went beyond Lasch in an intensive study of the relationship between the "family professionals" and American society in the interwar years. According to her, these newly minted professionals

> believed that the findings of the new sciences would ultimately enable them to pro-
> duce a managed society, an ideology that historians and others have labeled "social
> engineering." This conviction led to the establishment of innumerable programs,
> agencies and services in both the public and private sectors. Federal programs of
> family life and parent education introduced broad segments of the population to
> the principles of child development and mental hygiene while colleges, churches
> and community agencies brought counseling services within the reach of all.[21]

The point is that child science was not simply the natural outgrowth of developments within psychology. Its creators thought of it as a policy science, even, in some cases, as a form of social amelioration. At the same time, however, scientists themselves resisted the more obvious social reform implications of their new discipline and worked diligently both to make child science professional and to produce reliable, scientifically based findings.

In the early stages of the development of child science and the emergence of family professionals, the emphasis was on the measurement of physical growth on the one hand and the prevention of social pathology such as juvenile delinquency on the other. In time, the emphasis of the child research centers shifted from physical growth to psychology and to the relationship between IQ and environment, while in child guidance clinics, the focus shifted from prevention to problem children.

The key figure in the development of child science was Lawrence K. Frank, who, when he began his work in the early 1920s, was a young recent graduate in economics from Columbia. He used the money of large foundations to carry out a design that at first emphasized the development of a science of the normal child and then sought to disseminate the findings of this new science throughout the nation as a way of improving children's lives and thereby ensuring the future health of the nation.[22]

The program of child science Lawrence K. Frank developed while he was working with the Laura Spelman Rockefeller Memorial included not only the development of science but also its popular dissemination. In 1963 Frank recalled:

> The Rockefeller Memorial decided to establish a number of Centers for the study
> of child growth and development as a way of contributing to the welfare of chil-

dren by providing more dependable understanding and knowledge of their growth and development, and hopefully, by influencing parents through a program of parent education, tied with these Centers, and also by bringing more understanding of children to the various professions; pediatrics, education, nursing, and education in general. The general theory of this whole movement was that we knew little or nothing about children and that a concerted and intensive study of their development would be of permanent advantage and would certainly forward all the numerous different agencies and programs for welfare of children in the United States.[23]

Thus these factors came together for Frank and the child scientists of the twenties. At first, the study of children was linked explicitly to child welfare (and Frank probably preferred to maintain that link), but if the study of children was going to gain academic respectability, it had to be more closely associated with science than with child welfare. Thus much of the money in the 1920s went to the development of child science itself, rather than to child-helping projects.

In 1924 there were three child research centers already in existence, the Merrill Palmer School in Detroit, the Yale Psycho Clinic, headed by Dr. Arnold Gesell, and the Iowa Child Welfare Research Station. Founded in 1917 at the University of Iowa in Iowa City, the Iowa Child Welfare Research Station was modeled on the Agricultural Experiment Station at Iowa State College in Ames. Assisted by Dr. Carl E. Seashore, dean of the graduate college and professor of psychology at Iowa, Iowa socialite and philanthropist Cora Bussey Hillis used her contacts with the state Women's Christian Temperance Union (WCTU) and the Iowa Federation of Women's Clubs to pressure the state legislature to establish the station and provide funding. In Hillis's view, the role of the station was to promote practical child saving, but Seashore and Bird T. Baldwin, the first director, saw it as a vehicle for promoting psychological research on children at the university. A grant from the WCTU and increased funding from the state enabled the station to add a preschool nursery for research purposes—the first of its kind in the country—in 1922. Soon afterward, the station began receiving grant money from the Laura Spelman Rockefeller Memorial—at first small amounts and then major funding during the 1920s.

With George Stoddard as director in the 1930s, the station was at the center of a major controversy involving the issue of the constancy of IQ in young children. Iowa researchers Beth Wellman and Harold Skeels found evidence to suggest that the IQs of children could be improved, but key figures in child development research led by Lewis Terman of Stanford and a student of G. Stanley Hall disagreed and were able to maintain the view of the fixity of IQ in young children. In the 1990s, research and the success of the Head Start program have led to renewed respect for the Iowa research in the 1930s.[24]

When the Iowa station was founded, the academic study of children was just beginning. Child Study, a program begun by G. Stanley Hall while he was at Clark University, had relied on the observations of nonscientists. Hall's own publications, including his monumental *Adolescence,* were not typically the result of carefully constructed empirical research. Nevertheless Hall had emphasized his "Recapitulation Theory," which held that the history of human society recapitulated the evolution of the human species. Although this evolutionary theory probably did not aid the rise of experimental psychology, it did provide justification for paying more attention to infants and children in psychology. Meanwhile, the new research methodology, borrowed from the traditions of German science and Wilhelm Wundt, the founder of modern psychology, took hold in academic psychology departments in the United States in the early twentieth century. Most of the major American psychologists of the early twentieth century studied with Wundt in Germany.[25]

In the early twentieth century, as a part of the cultural focus on children that was central to the Progressive Era, a number books about babies and their growth appeared. Of these, *Mental Development in the Child and the Race,* by James Mark Baldwin, a key figure in the early history of American psychology, and Millicent Shinn's *The Biography of a Baby* were the most significant. "All those who have given even casual observation to the doings of the nursery," Baldwin wrote,

> have been impressed with the extraordinary fertility of the child mind, from the second year onward, in imagining and plotting social and dramatic situations. It has not been as evident, however, to these casual observers, nor to many really more skilled, that they were observing in these fancy-plays the putting together anew of fragments, or larger pieces of their own mental history.[26]

Shinn, who called her approach biographical, claimed that she was looking at children younger than those considered in other studies. In his *Historical Introduction to Modern Psychology,* Gardiner Murphy calls *The Biography of a Baby* "a great landmark of simple, faithful, well-proportioned observations of a child's growth."[27]

From Baldwin, Shinn, and Hall came a psychological focus on children. That focus became more explicitly scientific because experimental psychology emerged as the dominant paradigm in the discipline and because the public responded favorably to some of the field's key figures, notably John Dewey, Edward L. Thorndike, and John B. Watson. The work of these three, at least in the public's mind, promised to unlock the secrets of the future. If the programs of Dewey, Thorndike, and Watson lived up to their advance billing, then Americans had the means to reshape their culture along whatever lines seemed best. Of the three, only Dewey had a clear vision of what those lines might be, but all three had found the means, they said, to make cultural change.

Dewey had established his reputation as a psychologist with the publication of a textbook in 1887 and a classic article, "The Reflex Article Concept in Psychology" in 1894, but he became famous not in psychology but in the emerging professional field of education. His most widely read book, *School and Society,* appeared in 1899. It was a series of lectures to the parents of the laboratory school of the University of Chicago explaining the curriculum and its underlying ideas. The essential process of education, Dewey explained, was "to lay hold upon the rudimentary instincts of human nature, and, by supplying a proper medium, so control their expression as . . . to facilitate and enrich the growth of the individual child." Dewey believed that by connecting themselves to life, schools would become instruments of social reform if the curriculum were based on psychological understanding of the child.[28]

Edward L. Thorndike was already at Columbia University when John Dewey moved there in 1904. Thorndike's first study, *Animal Intelligence,* published in 1898, had established his reputation as a leading figure in the stimulus-response approach to the study of learning. Thorndike disagreed vigorously with Dewey's ideas and approach. In *Educational Psychology,* Thorndike directly challenged Dewey's philosophy. "The one thing that educational theorists of today seem to place as the foremost duty of the schools— the development of powers and capacities," he wrote, "is the one thing that the schools or any other educational forces can do least." For Thorndike, the schools were sorters, rather than molders, of students. Schools "help society in general tremendously by providing it not with better men, but with the knowledge of which men are good."[29] Thus Thorndike became an early and enthusiastic supporter of using standardized tests to identify superior students.

Thorndike and John B. Watson had a great deal in common. Both had done early work with animals, and both believed in the stimulus-response approach to learning, but whereas Thorndike came down on the hereditarian side of the long-running nature-nurture controversy, Watson believed strongly in the power of conditioning—in a behavioral approach to psychology and child rearing. Never one to hold back, Watson claimed he could take any child and turn him (never her) into a genius. He wrote for the public rather than for other psychologists, and his works were not based on laboratory research. *Behavior: An Introduction to Comparative Psychology* established his reputation, and *Psychology from the Standpoint of a Behaviorist* was his first textbook. In 1928 his *Psychological Care of the Infant and Child* made him a leading expert on child rearing. For many academic psychologists, however, Watsonian behaviorism seemed more an applied aspect of the science rather than its future direction. And Watson was forced to leave the academy because of marital troubles. Although some of the research done at the Iowa Station tested some of his provisions, Watsonian behaviorism was already waning when the Laura Spelman Rockefeller Memorial money came to Iowa in 1925, though Watson's popular influence would continue for some time.[30]

Watson's child-rearing advice appeared in popular magazines and in his book, which was as much an attack on mothers as it was a manual of care. According to historian Nancy P. Weiss, Watson's advice was similar to that given in *Infant Care,* the child-rearing advice manual published by the Federal Children's Bureau. But, Weiss continues,

> In Watson, toilet training is early, habits are critical, crying infants are allowed to cry, scheduling must be maintained at all costs, and indulgence is frowned on, all of which can be found in early *Infant Care.* What changes is the attitude towards the caregiver: the mother in Watson is an impediment to the scientific upbringing of the young.[31]

Thus, after World War I, the stage was set for new developments in child science. In 1921 at Stanford the Commonwealth Fund had begun its support of Lewis Terman's project "Genetic Studies of Genius." Terman was doing a longitudinal study of 1,000 California children who had exceptionally high IQ scores. At Yale, Arnold Gesell, one of Hall's most prolific students, was busy measuring infants and children and turning out books such as *The Mental Growth of the Preschool Child* and *Infancy and Growth.* For Gesell, maturation and growth took place along predetermined paths and explained human development. Both Terman and Gesell rejected the total environmentalism— the idea that all behavior is learned—of Watson in favor of a much more hereditarian view. Genius, in Terman's view, was genetic, inherited, and not the product of environmental influences. A corollary of this viewpoint was the idea that IQ—the measure of intelligence, according to some psychologists in the period—was a fixed property that could not be influenced by environment.

Others, perhaps with different agendas, began to argue in the 1920s that a child's IQ could be changed. For example, Helen Thompson Woolley, a psychologist at the Merrill Palmer School in Detroit, found that the IQs of children improved in nursery school. Her findings had little impact, however, because she seemed in effect to be using IQ tests as a way of recruiting for the school.

Responding to Woolley, Florence Goodenough, recently hired at the Institute of Child Welfare of the University of Minnesota, another of the child science institutes formed with Laura Spelman Rockefeller Memorial money, reported in her own study that "spurious" factors might have contributed to the effect Woolley claimed. Goodenough, a student of Terman's, staunchly supported her mentor's view. In 1931 Goodenough and John Anderson, the director of the Minnesota institute, published *Experimental Child Study,* a work that was a major salvo in the continuing IQ wars and that historian Hamilton Cravens has labeled "a blueprint for determinism."[32]

Meanwhile, at another of Frank's sites, the Institute of Child Welfare at the University of California, psychologist Nancy Bayley began her own longitudinal study. Bayley found the kind of variation in IQ scores to which Woolley had alluded. "I was distressed to find that the IQ (the so called IQ) in these babies was not constant," she later recalled, "that the test scores in the first months were just unrelated to scores later on." Her conclusion was that early scores were unreliable and therefore not a sufficient basis for argument about the permanency of IQ.[33]

Wayne Dennis, one of the more prominent graduates in psychology from Clark, recalled that

When I first entered child psychology the emphasis on maturation was dominant; and, of course, maturation has a very decided role. Gesell's emphasis was on maturation although he certainly did also believe in environmental influences. What the data on institutional children showed me is that the influence of environment, (also of my data on drawings), that the influence of environment on intellectual development is very, very much greater than I would ever have supposed.[34]

J. McVickar Hunt, another psychologist active in the period, recalled that the real breakthrough in the struggle over the fixity of IQ came from Iowa researchers:

At about this same time through the '30s, the group at Iowa were very much concerned about the importance of experience in intellectual development. This group included Harold Skeels, Marie Skodak, and Beth Welman, who constituted the principal people on the staff of the Child Welfare Research Station, directed by George Dinsmore Stoddard. This group had seen retardation associated with orphanage rearing. In the '30s, this retardation was attributed to genetic constitution. The assumption was that those children who remained in the orphanage were unattractive and retarded, and this was why they remained in the orphanage. It was the merit of Skeels and Skodak and Welman to show that a nursery school that gave these children an opportunity to play with things and to get—interact with teachers and other people resulted in quite rapid growth and development while the nursery school was under way.[35]

The Iowa researchers had demonstrated, at least to their own satisfaction, that a child's IQ could be improved.

At the Child Welfare Institute at the University of California–Berkeley, the variations Nancy Bayley had discussed steadily attracted the notice of the researchers, even though during the 1930s, Terman and his followers had continued to maintain the fixity of IQ and to downplay the findings of Woolley, the Iowa Station researchers, and the results from California. According to Institute psychologist Jean W. Macfarlane, "We did get a tremendous amount of variability during the pre-school years, especially the early ones which, of course, was partly due to different developmental ratings, cooperation, health, and nature of test items." Despite Macfarlane's dismissive comment, when she reported at the annual meeting of the National Association for Nursery Education that the IQs of young children could be changed by environmental influences, her announcement made the newspapers. Macfarlane reported some wildly disparate scores in individual children, and the *Oakland Tribune* (October 31, 1939) explained that the reasons for these changes were that overanxious parents forced "children to accept a pace for which they are not suited and the failure of professional parent-substitutes to give proper relief to harassed mothers and fathers."[36] At the same conference, George Stoddard of the Iowa Child Research Station told the conferees that

> illegitimate children of a large sampling of dull and feeble-minded mothers and out-of-work or laboring-class fathers, if placed in good homes in early infancy, will turn out to be bright children as measured by the best test now available.

The paper was duly impressed, noting that

> To educators and citizens who were brought up to believe that nothing could be done with the Jukes and Kallikaks of the world these well-established findings, conducted for several years at Iowa, will come as something of a shock.

And the paper saw the implications:

> The possibility of increasing Intelligence Quotients of human beings through the improvement of economic conditions and through more mature emotional adjustments to reality opens the way for a better order of social life.[37]

Although the public was enthusiastic about the new possibilities, Terman and his supporters continued to believe that their view was essentially correct.

In 1971 the psychologists at the Institute of Human Development at the University of California–Berkeley (formerly the Institute of Child Welfare) acknowledged that their own work had challenged the conventional wisdom of the 1920s that mental ability was inherited. The situation, Bayley concluded in 1970, was that "the complex interaction of genetic potential and environmental stimulation in the context of maturing and pliable neural structures presents a setting in which the exact expression of mental abilities may be impossible to predict."[38] The public was attracted to the idea that something could be done to improve children's mental abilities. Just what might be done depended on what the child experts might communicate.

Not only psychologists studied children. Also notable was the work of the anthropologist Margaret Mead. Her study of adolescent girls in Samoa and New Guinea contradicted the prevailing wisdom in the United States that adolescence was a time of stress and emotional distress. In the late 1930s, there were a number of field studies of "primitive" children similar in scope to Mead's work; the most notable was one by psychologist Wayne Dennis on Hopi children.[39]

Although the development of a new science was paramount in the minds of the academics associated with the early days of the child development movement, there was an applied child welfare dimension—parent education, the process whereby scientific findings would be communicated to the general public. Implicit in Lawrence K. Frank's original design was the view that some parents (notably immigrants, urban working classes, and all African-Americans) needed expert advice about how to raise their children in a modern urban and industrial society. Ironically, the parents who responded most enthusiastically were well-off and middle class—the very ones who needed it least, according to Frank and other advocates. As the design evolved, most scientists concentrated on research and academic publication and left the public distribution of their findings to other professionals and popularizers.

As child science expanded and became more professionalized, a certain disdain for ordinary parents emerged. For example, one educational psychologist wrote the following about the parents of nursery school children:

Many parents, willing as they may be to assume the entire responsibility, are unfitted for the task of presenting the proper kind of stimulation and example for the child. Since the behavior of parents is frequently inadequate, and their personalities may be anything but balanced, the example they set for their children is an unfortunate one. All of this leads to the assertion that the needs of the child of today are adequately met by parents so seldom that it is necessary for the larger social group to become interested in the welfare of children before their personalities have become too definitely set in the wrong direction.[40]

When academics talked directly to laypeople, they frequently made an effort to "talk down" to their audiences. For example, before a 1939 conference of nursery school editors, a member of the program committee warned Jean Macfarlane:

The group attending the conference will be 80 percent what you might call lay people in the field of nursery education. If you look at the enclosed announcement you will see that you are addressing a group of day nursery workers—people who are interested in providing the right housing for young children; parents; and people working with parents; and groups of people who are interested in community projects which provide recreational facilities for young children; directors and assistants in camps, nurses and individuals working in the field of public health programs, as well as teachers in nursery schools. In many cases the psychological and psychiatric background of the latter is as scant as the groups I have mentioned above. . . . When you are talking to a day nursery matron or a social worker, or a director on the board of a day nursery, then you will need to speak in the simplest language possible.[41]

Macfarlane was willing to tone her remarks down. "I have just received your letter of Oct. 5," she wrote,

> and can revamp my vocabulary to suit a lay group, although I must admit that I had no idea the group would be as lay as you imply. I have had considerable experience in talking to PTA and boarding mother groups so it will be no wrench. . . . I have a through-going conviction that anything which is worth saying about human beings can be said simply.[42]

What had prompted this exchange was Emma Johnson's memory of the previous conference, where Lawrence K. Frank had spoken: "I hark back to two years ago when Lawrence Frank presented his paper on 'The Fundamental Needs of the Child,' " Johnson wrote to Macfarlane. "I enjoyed every minute of it, and felt it was just what we needed, but all through the audience came comments. . . . 'Fine! but over the heads of 90 percent.' True that was in Nashville, Tenn., and there was a large group of W. P. A. and Nursery school teachers and supervisors."[43] A variety of ideas about how parent education might be accomplished emerged in the period, including high school and college courses, study clubs, magazines and radio talks, and the use of nursery schools.

One proponent of using nursery schools to reach parents was Arnold Gesell. In 1926, at a conference sponsored by the Chicago Association for Child Study and Parent Education, Gesell argued:

> At present the developed mental welfare of this large number of children is very much at the mercy of individual homes, and of the mothers and fathers who help to make and sometimes mar those homes, so that the discovery of the pre-school child has resulted in a kind of rediscovery of the parent and we are beginning to sense also the tremendous social significance of the parent who, like the pre-school child, is now become something of a social problem. . . . The pre-school child as such scarcely exits. He is almost an abstraction, and if we are going to bring, as we must, this period of childhood under systematic control, social control, we must do it through measures of parent guidance, of adult and adolescent guidance, schemes of parental education, such as we have not even dreamed about, because there is no other way in which this complicated and enormous field can be brought under genuine and safe control.[44]

Gesell saw the creation and expansion of nursery schools as the primary means to accomplish these ends in a way that did not threaten the home: "The nursery school at present is simply on the skirmishing line, and it must be used as a method of developing and defining techniques of parental guidance, and pre-parental education." The beauty of this device, he concluded, was that "if we use it in that way we shall not in any sense weaken the home, but we shall strengthen the home." Parent education was necessary because of myriad threats to American civilization: crime, divorce, insanity, and a lower birthrate. Thus, he concluded, "We must find means of strengthening the psychological stamina of the next generation. And if we must find means we shall get back to the very beginning of things, to the cradle and that is the reason that science is taking and that scientific studies are taking new shape."[45]

Nursery school children's parents seemed very interested in the education offered to them by the teachers and administrators of the schools. Just as Gesell had argued, nursery schools were good recruiting devices for parents to educate. At the Institute for Child Welfare associated with the University of California–Berkeley, parents were invited to a series of five meetings "to discuss the issues and practical problems a parent is confronted with in, to put it baldly, making his child fit to live with." The first three meetings were devoted to "the behavior patterns infants and young children are required to learn in connection with satisfying their needs for food, sleep and elimination." The other two dealt with "the child's relationships with other children and with adults."[46] Most parents who sought nursery schools for their children were eager for further education. A nursery school director reported in 1932 that "nearly all of the mothers cooperate to the best of their ability, but the process of learning how is long and slow."[47]

Parents were not coerced into participating in the educational programs of the nursery schools, but the way nursery school workers treated them and their relative influence over the curriculum depended in large measure on their levels of education and income. Even though parent education was widely available through the nursery schools of the 1930s, family professionals and some child scientists wanted to expand its scope. At the 1930 White House Conference on Children, Dr. Martha Van Rensselaer, director of the College of Home Economics at Cornell, called for more parent education for middle-class parents:

> The advice of Aunt Hilda and the neighbors has been proven unsafe. Even physicians differ among themselves. The psychology learned at school does not work when the baby has a temper tantrum. . . .
>
> So much has happened, so much has been found out lately, times have changed so swiftly in relationship to old guides and directions, that parents must go back to school and resume the learning which some of them thought forever completed.[48]

And others at the conference indicated that immigrants and African-Americans should be targeted for more parent education.[49]

Another way in which parent education took place was over the radio and in syndicated newspaper columns by well-known personalities such as Angelo Patri. He wrote newspaper columns from 1923 to 1962 and spoke on radio programs from 1928 to 1943. He claimed he received thousands of letters each month from troubled parents, thus documenting strong parental interest in the new expertise. An immigrant from Italy, Patri himself had taken courses at Columbia from John Dewey and had been a school administrator in New York City. For the most part, Patri offered nonjudgmental, common-sense advice, but he dealt mostly with older children and was very sympathetic to children's needs, at times taking the child's viewpoint instead of the parents. The following is an example from a radio program broadcast in December 1931 in which Patri reads a letter from a 15-year-old girl whose father became angry when a boy walked her home:

> the girl whose father roars at the sight of a boy in the house knows that father is wrong. She knows that there is nothing to fear where she and that boy are concerned. She knows that father's attitude is unreasoning and absurd. But father does not know that he will be the last one to whom she will go in time of need. He does not know that she will evade him and he will become a stranger to his own child.[50]

Patri was not unsympathetic to parents, however. "No child can bring himself up," he said in November 1931, "and make a success of it."[51]

Patri's long run as a columnist and radio broadcaster illustrates an important point—much of the information about children that parents sought and used was popular, rather than academic. Lawrence K. Frank had conceived of a popular magazine to transmit the findings of the new child science. Frank found an ingenious way to raise money for the start-up of the magazine by giving money to universities, who in turn bought stock in the magazine. In 1972 George Hecht, the longtime publisher of *Parents' Magazine,* recalled some of the ideas and practices that had characterized the magazine in the twenties and thirties:

> The main concern of parents were problems of sex education and discipline, and suitable recreation for children. Many parents looked to *Parents' Magazine* for guidance in how to feed their children, to feed them the most nutritious foods. We also gave them guidance about games that could be played at home and in playgrounds by the children. We gave them guidance as to what motion pictures to take their children to. Throughout the decade that has been a problem that is worried about in every home.

Although the magazine had been set up to transmit the new knowledge, things did not quite work that way, as Hecht continued:

> Many of the child development researchers in universities throughout the country got in touch with us when we started the magazine, and some of them sent us articles, but we found that we couldn't use many of those articles because they were not interestingly enough written. They didn't have sufficient application.

Sometimes the editors "rewrote the articles and resubmitted them to the authors" to make sure the technical points were correct. The better articles did not come from experts, though: "We found that we would get better and more useful articles" from "just average mothers" who were "intelligent" and "who had [had] successful experiences with their own children." *Parents'*

Magazine became an enormous success.[52] And Hecht and *Parents Magazine'* had learned to listen to mothers.

Mothers were anything but passive consumers. In the 1920s and 1930s, the Home Economics Extension Service of the Agriculture Department maintained home bureaus in rural parts of New York, Iowa, and Minnesota to provide mothers with the latest information about the new child sciences as well as about child health and nutrition. In New York, Cornell University, aided by a grant from the Laura Spelman Rockefeller Memorial, set up a series of child study clubs beginning in 1925. These clubs met to discuss materials and information sent to them by Cornell. The groups, though designed to be rural, were popular in all parts of the state, including city suburbs.

In these groups, the experiences of real life and the theories of the experts came face-to-face. In some cases, mothers rejected the advice that crying infants be left alone (this was part of the habit training recommended by the Children's Bureau's *Infant Care* and derived from John B. Watson's recommendations). In the minutes taken after a meeting, the agent remarked: "One woman ruined meeting by insisting on giving her ideas about kindness to children, which were thoroughly sentimental and selfish." The agent was outraged by this display and concluded her minutes: "Her main idea was that if a baby cried it needed picking up, that it was lonely!" But mothers could be appreciative of the advice, too, especially the notion that babies could be toilet trained at an early age. They worried, however, about whether the early years of a child's life were crucial in determining the child's future, some mothers rejecting the total environmentalism of John B. Watson, and others accepting it. Finally, mothers brought their own expertise, especially when it came to discipline, to the clubs. The experts frowned on physical punishment, but mothers cited circumstances in which they believed swift physical punishment was appropriate.[53]

Still other forms of parent education took place in college classrooms, where students, mostly young women, learned the basics of child care. One of the early child experts, Myrtle McCraw, a New York psychologist, recalled that when she taught basic human development to college girls, they were very nervous when holding babies. McCraw believed that the fad of behaviorism, as preached by Watson, was partly to blame: "The behaviorists hurt us by not giving proper respect for direct observation in the early days," she recalled. She also saw that the modern age had disrupted old familial patterns—such as the process of learning how to deal with babies; she wanted to educate the young women not in terms of fixed conclusions but in terms of getting them "to cultivate their own observational acuity, not just measuring." By doing so, she hoped to "recapture some of the advantages of the kinship family."[54] Thus parent education was not only a matter of indoctrination; it was also an effort to "parent" those whose own experiences had been limited.

By the end of the 1930s, a number of changes in the child science and child therapy continuum had taken place. Parent education, once mainly a design advocated by Lawrence Frank or Arnold Gesell, had become commonplace. The Federal Children's Bureau, the home economics extension programs at Cornell, radio programs, the Child Study Association, *Parents' Magazine,* and the nursery schools (now sponsored by the federal Works Progress Administration) actively disseminated information and advice about how to care for children. As this system expanded in response to demands from the parents themselves, its content and emphasis changed. In the 1920s, as Frank and Gesell indicated, Americans were worried about social pathology and immigrant families. By the 1930s, they were concerned with the economy and the rise of fascism in Europe. In the late 1930s, expert advice on families and children emphasized democracy, and the 1940 White House Conference significantly was on Children and Youth in a Democracy. The key to democracy, said the experts, was family life itself, and they stood ready to help meet the new threat. In a manuscript entitled "Democracy Begins at Home," Arnold Gesell spelled out the role for experts:

> The further evolution of democracy demands a much more refined understanding of infants and preschool children than our civilization has yet attained. Should science ever arrive at the happy juncture where it can focus its full force upon the interpretation of life, it will enable us to do more complete and timely justice to the individual personality in the very young. And this in turn will have a humanizing affect [sic] upon the adult population. . . . Only through a democratically conceived system of developmental supervision can we attain a more just and universal distribution of developmental opportunity for infants and preschool children. The scientific study of child development has already given us new insights into the manner in which the mind grows and takes shape. This knowledge is ready for application on a wider social scale. Science needs deeper application to make democracy a more assured possession.[55]

Although Gesell had been prescient in his vision of nursery schools as vehicles for parent education, his notion that democracy depended on child scientists and their expertise went too far, as no less a personage than Lawrence K. Frank indicated. It was not that Frank had given up on his ideas about social reform through child science, but rather that the retention of democracy also depended on democratic means. The slowness and inefficiency of democratic governments bothered Willard Beatty, chair of the Progressive Education Association. In a letter to Frank in 1938, Beatty complained that "autocratic governments secure prompt changes in their educational systems," but "if social progress in the United States is not to be retarded, in comparison with progress in autocracies, some democratic procedures must be utilized to speed up the adoption by our secondary schools of educational practices recognized to be sound."[56] Beyond this, Beatty wanted better family life education and wanted to complain about the unfair advantage dictators had.

> We are urged to adopt the scientific method as the procedure to solve all problems, to exalt "reason above all else"; to rely solely upon religious beliefs and faith,

while abroad the dictators demand loyalty and obedience and the sacrifice of the individual to the state which lives by force.

Beatty also wanted more instruction in the arts and more awareness of the importance of the arts in shaping social values:

> The creation of new sensibilities and their diffusion throughout a society is primarily the task of the artist whose sensitive awareness makes him respond to the human aspects of life that are ignored or despised by others. It is the artist who portrays these human values and communicates them through esthetic [sic] experience wherein the individual may feel and vicariously experience what life really means to others.[57]

But, Frank reminded Beatty, changing the schools in the United States was all but impossible because of entrenched interests and competing professional organizations.

Thus, as America stood ready to enter World War II, the study of children had expanded dramatically. A new discipline, child development, had been brought into existence since the Great War, and a new professional organization, the Society for Research in Child Development, had been created in 1934. Similarly, a series of child guidance clinics, designed to remedy social ills using the new mental sciences, appeared in the early 1920s and formed their professional organization, the American Orthopsychiatric Association, in 1924. By the end of the 1930s, however, much of the early promise of child science was gone. Child science became more an academic than a popular phenomenon, and although much of the shape and most of the institutions of Lawrence K. Frank's design remained, the idealism and hope of the early years were gone, perhaps destroyed in the devastation of the Great Depression. Parent education was alive and thriving. Child science was in the process of weathering its first great crisis—the battle over IQ—and most child guidance clinics preferred to deal with problem children rather than social problems. Yet the scientific study of children continued to grow, even as it was no longer tied to a large-scale vision of social improvement. By the end of the 1930s, child science was important in its own right. In 1964 Jean Macfarlane wrote to Lawrence K. Frank on his 75th birthday:

> Our babies, now age 35 with many children of their own, have forced us to abandon or to make drastic modification of our pet theoretical convictions. A large proportion of them just irresponsibly ignored too many of our well-documented predictions. And you, Mr. Lawrence K. Frank, by your fostering of our longitudinal studies can just accept the responsibility for our humiliation and our fun.[58]

In a sense, she spoke for all her colleagues: "Pet theoretical convictions" had to give way to the results from experience and research. Between the wars, child science had come of age.

6

Children and Social Agencies

There was a tremendous growth in the work of social agencies and in social work during the 1920s. With the coming of the depression, local agencies contracted, but federally sponsored ones expanded. The increase of social awareness associated with the Progressive Era did not continue after World War I, but social services for children were an exception to this rule. The Children's Bureau, established in 1912, broadened its mission as it supported legislation against child labor, helped to sponsor the Sheppard-Towner Act that provided preventative health care to pregnant women and to infants, and drafted the parts of the Social Security Act that pertained to women. Similarly, public interest in the scientific study of children grew, and several large foundations gave money for that purpose. The Commonwealth Fund gave money for the development of child guidance clinics, and the Laura Spelman Rockefeller Memorial supported academic research regarding children.

Additionally, the number of juvenile courts increased, and with them came the expansion of social services for children. Social casework became the standard approach to family problems and to problems associated with children. Similarly, public schools and compulsory school attendance laws had become universal by the 1930s. Schools were also expanding their offerings, so that high schools were now widely available as well. School attendance increased, too, and with the growth of schools came other social services—schools had social workers or visiting teachers who inquired into home life, and they also offered psychological testing services. So far as children were concerned, then, the period between the wars was a time of the expansion of services. The depression curtailed the services temporarily, but most were restored during the 1930s. This chapter will trace the growth of children's services during these two decades and inquire into their mode of functioning.[1]

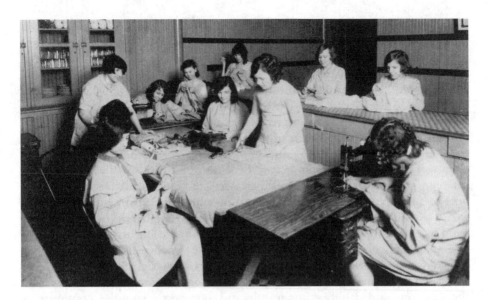

Sewing class, Sophie Wright Settlement, Detroit, Michigan (ca. 1937). (Photographer unknown. Bentley Historical Library, Ann Arbor, Michigan, Children's Fund Papers, Box 18.)

In the nineteenth century, various private charities and philanthropies combined themselves into Charity Organization Societies to eliminate "double dipping" among their clients and to ensure that aid went to the deserving. Charities called this practice "scientific philanthropy," and the modern practice of social work evolved from it. Implicit in both the organizations and the processes employed was the idea that the recipients of charity required close scrutiny and that the aid was an act of charity and generosity and not in any sense an entitlement. By the 1920s, most charity organization societies had renamed themselves Family Service Associations or some similar label.[2]

Agencies believed that they acted in the best interests of their clients and that doing so gave them the right to dispense unsolicited advice and to intervene directly in the lives of the less fortunate. Most of the staff at the agencies were professionals (social workers were the dominant type, but there were also psychologists and physicians) and thus were well educated and salaried.[3] Sometimes clients objected, but few families seeking aid could afford to turn caseworkers away. In Cleveland caseworkers reported on their difficulties in regular meetings. The February 6, 1920, minutes of the Home Economics Committee of the Cleveland Family Service Association revealed a continuing concern with children's health (the committee hoped to measure weight gain and monitor milk consumption) and with the way one client was managing her money. The caseworker indicated that she planned to visit a problem family "to try to get the woman to keep household accounts and show wherein

she could not live within her present income. It was also suggested that the
boarders be asked to pay an additional amount for their laundry, as the rate
for all expenses seems entirely too small." In March the committee heard a
report on a successful program in New York where children were weighed
"and the mothers instructed in improving the food and health habits of the
children."[4] After World War I, Americans had become obsessed with children's health and their rates of growth because so many young men had been
released from the draft because of their poor physical condition.

The Home Economics Committee decided in March 1920 to set up a
demonstration nutrition clinic for 15 children to show the relationship
between good nutrition and health. In April the committee terminated support to a family because of the husband's gambling and drinking and decided
to ask the husband's employer, who had endorsed the check, where the husband was getting his liquor. In April the committee heard about a social
worker who worked through the schools in New Orleans, conducting nutrition classes and visiting children in their homes when they were ill. In Cleveland the nutrition classes began in June but soon ran into difficulties because
the children and families apparently did not appreciate the committee's
efforts on their behalf:

> Miss Schroeder in her work with nutrition classes has come up against the problem
> of lack of discipline in the homes of our families. She asked whether A. C. [Associ-
> ated Charities] should consider organizing groups of mothers to study child train-
> ing. The committee agreed that some pressure should be brought to bear on Moth-
> ers' Clubs and settlements for this sort of class, but the members doubted if it were
> wise for A. C. to start group meetings. It was suggested that speakers be asked to
> present our staff some of the essentials of discipline from time to time. The com-
> mittee agree that a resolution be sent from the A. C. to certain schools and settle-
> ments urging the consideration of this subject in their material for Mothers' Clubs.

Still, the committee members persisted with their club, and by October it had
evolved into a sort of little homemakers' club that encouraged children to begin
preparing wholesome meals at home. The committee finally found a way to
convince mothers of the importance of diet by holding classes in hospitals.
There doctors with their white coats and charts made a strong impression.[5]

Although the caseworkers might have been intrusive and superior, they
sometimes uncovered major problems affecting the lives and safety of children. In November 1920, the minutes of the Home Economics Committee
noted:

> Miss Schroeder presented a family problem involving a man, woman, and six chil-
> dren, the oldest of whom is a 15 year old girl. The woman goes out to work some
> and claims that she has to because her husband's wages are not enough to keep the
> family. The house and children show signs of neglect. It was suggested that a men-

Mothers' club, Sophie Wright Settlement, Detroit, Michigan (ca. 1937). (Photographer unknown. Bentley Historical Library, Ann Arbor, Michigan, Children's Fund Papers, Box 18.)

tal test be given the woman, if possible in her home, and that a definite stand be taken on cleaning up the house, possibly by inaugurating a house-cleaning week and furnishing paint if necessary. It was also suggested that the Visitor see the teachers of the children so that the committee would know more about the individual attention necessary.

The committee continued to worry about how to deliver the message about proper child management to client families. Part of the difficulty was cultural, and part had to do with differing sensibilities. In March,

> Miss Day presented a family in which problems of nourishment, housekeeping and discipline are dominant. The widowed mother is an Italian woman, who is very ignorant of American ways. Rose, ten, and the oldest is underweight. Two younger girls and one boy are over-weight because of bad eating habits. The woman is slow to learn and carry out suggestions. She formerly punished the children cruelly and after being convinced that she must not do this, has little control.

The committee again suggested a mental test and also the idea of affiliation with a mother's club. In the case of this family and others, the committee also worried about children getting enough fresh air and sufficient mental stimulation.[6]

The caseworkers from the Cleveland Family Service Association found many conflicts between parents and children. In some cases, children wanted "American" style foods instead of the traditional fare of their immigrant parents' homeland. Many children had to work, and they sometimes resented having to give up their earnings for the family. Daughters especially wanted spending money for clothes and hats. The committee responded to this concern by drawing up recommended budgets for working girls—with almost no allowance for entertainment and adornment. They drew up budgets for boys, too, with different allocations.[7]

When caseworkers found children being physically abused, they acted quickly to remove them to institutions. In cases of malnutrition, caseworkers sought physical examination through the schools, and if they could not persuade the parents to deal with the problem (sometimes using church influence), they would petition the juvenile court to intervene. They would also try to maintain close contact with families where children seemed to be neglected or poorly fed. In some cases, caseworkers would put children in day care so that the mother could turn her attention to proper housekeeping. When children were in their late teens, the committee favored putting them to work instead of using scarce agency funds to keep them in school.[8]

Given the tendency of single young people in the city to amuse themselves in ways middle-class social workers found unacceptable, another area social agencies worried about was leisure time. George Bellamy of Hiram House, a Cleveland settlement, spoke to the Home Economics Committee on February 8, 1924, about the issue. He warned against the waste of leisure time and said that the city was full of unsavory amusements that were the cause of moral decay. He saw the role of Hiram House as building character by building up young people's resistance to evil. "The problem of society is to make the environment contribute to right development of the instincts," he said. He stressed the importance of play in teaching young people how to live and work in groups. Play, he argued, promoted a sense of honesty and justice.[9]

The committee continued to worry about young people in the city and especially about the wages of working girls. Showing some sympathy for the difficulties working girls faced, the committee minutes nevertheless reflected the general sentiment that girls worked only for frills and not to support themselves. Yet the committee members (no doubt reflecting on their own situations) did cast a vote for the independence of working girls, noting that "it is better for a girl to work than to have her father support her." The committee felt that girls should be able to earn enough to live decently and with dignity. They reacted strongly when they learned that a factory girl in Dayton had won a prize for the budget she drew up for her weekly salary of $16: "Miss McLeod felt that instead of wasting her time and energy trying to budget such a small income, it would have been better for the girl to get enough education so she could earn more money."[10]

Boys' basketball team, Sophie Wright Settlement, Detroit, Michigan (ca. 1937). (Photographer unknown. Bentley Historical Library, Ann Arbor, Michigan, Children's Fund Papers, Box 18.)

Underlying these discussions about recreation, leisure, and the wages of the working girls was considerable concern about sexuality. In May 1924, one Reverend Barry spoke to the committee about the church's role in sex education. "The church ought to help boys and girls with their problems of sex relationships," he said. "Sex knowledge in itself may be dangerous, but the church has an opportunity to surround it with religious and holy ideals and thus take away the dangerous element." The reason the church had to take this step was that the family was breaking down, and as a result, "parents do not have a guiding moral influence over their children." It was not that parents themselves lacked morals but rather that in modern life, "it is very difficult to convince the children on this point."[11]

Another Cleveland agency that worried about the lives of young women in the city was the Women's Protective Association, an organization that worked closely with the Cleveland police. Organized in 1917 to protect young women, the association operated a separate detention home for young women throughout the 1920s and provided some social casework for the young women who had come to the attention of the police. In 1924 the association explained that "It assists girls fallen below the accepted moral standards, counsels parents as to methods of discipline and locates run away and missing girls." The association claimed it was helping girls develop higher moral standards, and for some, it provided a second chance. "The Women's Protective Association endeavors to help the girl, thru her difficulties and make the necessary adjustments," they said, "in order for her to take her place in society." But, they added, theirs was a large task because "there is ground for belief that large numbers of girls are morally lax." The reason for this was that "many girls of this class sacrifice themselves for a good time or for parents in the shape of jewelry and clothes. It is the universal experience that the girl who falls almost finds it impossible to regain her self respect where she is known."

The association saw itself working with three kinds of girls: those who were mentally deficient; those who were irresponsible and had "no moral standards, no moral stability"; and the vicious type, "persons possessed of the very devil." Agreeing with the Reverend Barry, they concluded that "young people of today get their information about courtship and home life and divorce from newspapers and moving pictures. As a result they regard lightly these things."[12] The church might engage in some preventative activity, but it was left to agencies such as the Women's Protective Association to pick up the pieces when protection failed.

The association did maintain a home for working girls, so their work had some preventative qualities, but they saw themselves as dealing with people who had very few chances. In 1922 the physician employed by the association explained why, in her opinion, the problems they faced were so difficult. "The Women's Protective Association deals very largely with the problems of families of low grade intelligence, and with many of neurotic tendencies, who find it difficult, and probably always will find it difficult," she contended, "to adjust themselves to the standards set by brighter and more stable people." "The main hope for people of this type," she continued, "is to get hold of them when they are young. The very hold which their bad habit has upon them indicates that the main problem is to train them young, so that if they do not act from reason or intelligence, they may at least keep out of serious trouble from force of habit." Dr. Eleanor Rowland Wembridge also referred to "the unsupervised behavior of young girls" and "the lack of understanding of immigrant parents of American ways, necessitating education of adults in American customs and ideals." In these sentiments, the doctor and the minister could agree. One reason social agencies such as the Women's Protective Association and the Family Service Association existed was to deal with the serious pathology some young people exhibited.[13]

One strategy the Women's Protective Association adopted was the Big Sister program. In 1923 the program's director reported, "we have about 28 big sisters and 29 little sisters. These girls represent all kinds of problems,—some of them were referred to the Women's Protective Ass'n because they had taken things from a department store,—some had run away from home,—others were unadjusted at school or in their homes." Mostly the Big

Sisters got the girls with minor problems. "So far," the director continued, "all of our girls have been referred by the Women's Protective Ass'n. Eventually, we hope to have them referred directly from the schools and by their parents."[14]

By the following year, the Big Sisters were having to deal with more than petty offenses, and they too said that children had to be dealt with at an earlier age if prevention was going to have any meaning. Still, the big sister program had its rewards—especially for the older women participants. According to Mildred Buttorf, the director:

> When a women of intelligence and education inserts herself in [the life of] an under-privileged girl her opportunities for beneficial influence are enormous. She can bridge the chasm of misunderstanding between mothers and daughters; her opportunity for character building perhaps exceeds any other in the social work field, . . . [it leads] to close personal contact, through which she can share the advantages, richness and varied interest which her life and experience has brought her. For the individual Big Sister, is not the sympathy, the courage and the desire to understand, an investment which yields large returns in growth and usefulness?[15]

The Big Sister program was joined by a medical program and a section that specialized in social casework. Many of the girls who were brought in by the police were runaways from nearby towns, although some of them probably had parental approval to come to the city to look for work.

The economy of Cleveland was booming in the middle twenties, and most of the girls who came looking for work found it. But the Women's Protective Association said this did not eliminate the possibilities of trouble. Small-town and farm parents had no idea what kinds of danger lay in wait for their sons and daughters. One of these dangers was the lack of wholesome recreation, a need other agencies had also noticed. Vigilance was needed, and "all our social activities should be supervised," said the director of the assistance program. "All of the lines of amusements, and every group of youth engaged in work of any kind should have a trained, sympathetic and wise counsellor." Public amusements were far too commercialized to be wholesome, so the director continued, "it is therefore our responsibility to provide places for play, for recreation, and amusements for the youth of today," places that would be "safe and wholesome."[16]

The Women's Protective Association also maintained a facility for working girls who could not find acceptable lodging. The Junior League of Cleveland, with some assistance from the Cleveland Fund, also maintained such a facility. The association staffers at their home tried to give the girls instruction in proper social graces, but this met with mixed results because some of the girls rejected this sort of help.[17]

These agencies tried to protect the morals of young women living and working in the city. At the same time, there was the belief that the girls them-

selves were responsible for any problems they might have, especially problems associated with sex. This view reflected the rise of a psychoanalytically
oriented view of women and a belief that young women behaved seductively
around men. Historian Linda Gordon argues that the rise of "female sexual
delinquency" in effect defined the victimization of young women out of existence. According to Gordon,

> Girls who stayed away from home, came home late, who used vulgar language,
> rode in cars, drank or smoked, walked or dressed "immodestly," were liable to be
> declared delinquent, and thereby deprived of sympathy if they were sexually vic-
> timized. A medical expert in sex-abuse cases insisted that "we seldom find cases of
> rape in healthy, robust girls in possession of their faculties and who are above the
> age of fourteen"—those who were healthy are presumed to have been willing.[18]

The Women's Protective Association understood at some level the nature of
the system and how it worked to label sexually active girls as delinquent, even
if they had been raped. The association sought to work to control the behavior of the girls instead of trying to change the system.

The Children's Aid Society of Cleveland, which like the Women's Protective Association maintained a home, was a very different sort of agency. Their
home was primarily for problem-plagued children. The society had revised
their constitution in 1928 because their earlier mission of providing care for
orphans had given way to other needs. Their new purpose was to set up industrial schools for "the benefit and proper education of the neglected, destitute,
and homeless children of Cleveland and its vicinity, and thus furnish them a
home until they can maintain themselves or be otherwise provided with suit-
able homes in families." The program began in 1923 as a mental study center
for needy children. In 1924 the Commonwealth Fund granted them money to
set up a demonstration clinic, and in 1927 the society operated a child guidance clinic. In addition to the home, the society provided medical examinations. After the funding for the clinic ended, the society continued to provide
psychological and medical examinations for troubled children.[19]

In an interview in 1937, Lawrence Cole, who became the superintendent
of the Children's Aid Society of Cleveland in 1928, explained:

> The Children's Aid Society has helped other social agencies find out why some
> children have trouble at home, in school, in boarding homes or institutions. Par-
> ents may seek institutional care for their children who disobey, run away, fight , or
> steal. These parents do not know why—they only know that they cannot put up
> with the trouble any longer. Agencies ask for the study of neglected and abused
> children to discover what damage may have been done to their body or personal-
> ity, and how best this damage can be corrected.[20]

Thus, although the cutting edge of guidance clinics had come and gone, the
Cleveland Children's Aid Society continued to provide services both to chil-

YWCA day nursery. A young man from the National Youth Administration (NYA) teaching children how to form clay figures, Washington, D.C. (ca. 1938). (Photographer unknown, NYA. National Archives Neg. 119-G-850-D.)

dren and to other agencies who dealt with children. Progressivism may have ended with World War I, but services to children did not.

One of the most important agencies working with youth was the YMCAs—for both young men and young women. The Detroit YMCAs were among the most active. There were several different branches in Detroit, but one central organization. In the 1920s, the Detroit Y maintained a "colored branch"—officially known as the St. Antoine Branch—and the central YMCA also ran its own school, which was described in the 1922–1923 annual report as "the only Protestant school in a city where the Catholic influences are strong educationally." The institution was in fact a very exclusive private school for privileged boys. Y leaders were proud of the fact that graduates went to prestigious eastern private colleges. The Y also ran an evening high school and claimed that its teachers taught character as well as skills. They were especially proud of their program for "handicapped men" and of "father and son week."

Another program aimed directly at high school students was the "Hi-Y's," which gave the students vocational guidance and emphasized uplifting reading and character building. High school principals gave these programs their full endorsement.[21]

The YMCA enjoyed strong national support at the highest levels. In 1925 President Coolidge and Herbert Hoover both gave the organization their blessings, Coolidge noting that "probably no other lay force asserts so large an influence upon the young people as that which you represent. It stands as a direct challenge to materialism. . . . It is a most practical effort in the training of citizenship." Hoover chimed in with similar sentiments, observing that the YMCA was "one of these great agencies of spiritual support. Its base is strongest in the cities, where the tests of modern society are most severe. You have the advantageous position in a normal approach to youth with its curious modern admixture of angles, inquiries, revolts and loyalties. Life goes the way youth finally takes."[22] Politicians liked the Y; it focused on character and citizenship, was comfortably Protestant, and did not challenge the dominant order of things. Hoover may have spoken for many in the nation as a whole. They were not really interested in Progressivism any more, but they still supported programs for youth, especially those programs that built character.

The Detroit Y ran two camps and claimed they were planning a third. In their annual report, they made no effort to hide the purposes of the camps:

> We are fortunate in having two camps—one, at Philip H. Gray Camp, which provides for the boy from the financially privileged home; and the other at Camp Ohiyesa, which is within the reach of the boy from the moderate home, as well as providing for the less fortunate boys. What we need now is a suitable site for the colored young men and boys, and an earnest effort is being made to secure such a place.[23]

The Y maintained a department for underprivileged boys and in 1929 claimed that "over 1,000 so-called underprivileged or limited membership boys were reached by the Association." The Detroit Y believed that they could "reach and serve this class of boys," and they thought opening new buildings would help in this effort. Things at the St. Antoine Branch were not going well, however. Attendance and membership began to decline in the late twenties. "Notwithstanding its fine equipment," the annual report noted in 1929, "this branch has found great difficulty in maintaining membership and in filling dormitory rooms especially, for the members of this race suffer first in any financial depression."[24]

The Y also sponsored "mothers and fathers" clubs. These clubs helped the Y to purchase small items such as radios and public address systems and was, according to the leadership, "drawing the Association and the home closer together." A group still neglected were "young men between school and marriage," and the Y needed to "adopt a policy which will enable us to give these 75,000 young men an opportunity to work together." So the Y saw itself as providing a wide range of services to young men and boys. It pro-

Manual training class, Sophie Wright Settlement, Detroit, Michigan (ca. 1937). (Photographer unknown. Bentley Historical Library, Ann Arbor, Michigan, Children's Fund Papers, Box 18.)

vided those services to poor boys and privileged ones alike, and it was proud of its services to African-Americans and aware in one sense of the difficulties they faced.[25]

Despite the pride the Detroit Y took in its services to African-American youth, those young people were much more likely to come under the auspices of the juvenile court. In New York City in the 1920s, in proportion to their numbers, African-American youth were twice as likely as white youth to be arraigned in the juvenile court. Once dealt with by the court, African-American youth received fewer services and were far less likely to be placed on probation than white children. As the Detroit Y had noted, urban African-Americans had already begun to suffer from unemployment well before the great stock market crash of 1929, the traditional starting point of the depression. Social services were not readily available to African-American children in any case. During the late twenties and throughout the thirties, the number of welfare agencies exclusively for African-American children did not increase, and many other private agencies refused to provide services to African-American children. Most city and state agencies in New York City were officially "color-blind," but in practice, they were reluctant to make services available to African-American children.

There were exceptions to this rule, however. The New York Children's Aid Society operated a branch in Harlem, and the Colored Orphans' Asylum continued to function during the depression, although under seriously overcrowded conditions. The Urban League sponsored various relief operations, such as Boy Scout troops and summer camps for children. The Utopia Children's House provided day care and after-school programs; they also provided a daily hot lunch during the depression years. Also central to the welfare of African-American families and children during the depression were the African-American churches, especially the Abyssinian Baptist Church, whose pastor was Adam Clayton Powell Sr. Churches routinely provided day care and relief.[26]

During the depression, African-Americans faced many kinds of discrimination. In New York the mayor's committee on unemployment donated funds for a separate summer camp for African-American children rather than force white camps to accept them. Similarly, the Children's Aid Society bought a camp for African-American children rather than send them to exclusively white camps. There were no public facilities for dependent and neglected children in New York, so the Children's Court relied on religious agencies for placement when children were removed from their homes. It was very difficult to find foster home placement for African-American children. One symptom of this difficulty was that children tended to remain longer in the Colored Orphans' Asylum as the depression deepened. Efforts to get other agencies to accept African-American orphans proved futile. One consequence of this was that judges were reluctant to declare African-American children neglected or abused.[27]

In 1937 the State Department of Social Welfare found conditions at the Colored Orphans' Asylum unacceptable—there were 800 children in its care—and as a result of the criticism, the orphanage reduced its population to 250. Because of this action, there was a serious lack of services for African-American children, and the Welfare Council of New York City set up the Standing Committee on Negro Welfare in 1938. The committee found that serious needs of African-American families and children were not being met. What made this all the more difficult was that the African-American population of New York more than doubled with no appreciable increase in social services. The New York Department of Public Welfare found recreational facilities for children in Harlem "inadequate and unsatisfactory." Meanwhile, African-American families coped with the depression and declining economic circumstances by using a variety of strategies. They took in lodgers, borrowed from friends and relatives, shared food and resources, engaged in barter, found ways to tap electric lines without paying, and in general coped and survived while receiving fewer services than many white people.[28]

Child guidance clinics appeared after World War I, their growth stimulated by grants from the Commonwealth Fund, and proliferated in the 1920s and continued throughout the depression years. The clinics' purpose could have been called social, but they also sought to apply psychological expertise—loosely defined—to the problems of children. The fund chose juvenile delinquency as its project and, much influenced by the mental hygiene movement (an effort to bring the insights of psychiatry into the community), decided on child guidance clinics as the method to combat delinquency. The fund worked closely with the New School for Social Research in New York and the National Committee on Mental Hygiene and its Division on the Prevention of Delinquency. That division and the Division of Visiting Teachers cooperated in developing a plan to train psychiatric social workers, who would become staff members at a series of clinics to be established. Two such clinics were already in existence: one run by Lightner Witmer in Philadelphia, and the Juvenile Psychopathic Institute in Chicago, headed by William A. Healy. The assumption behind this initiative was that juvenile delinquency was psychological in origin and could be either cured or prevented using the techniques of psychoanalysis.

Teachers were to be recruited into the enterprise so that they could spot potential delinquents. Meanwhile more social workers and analytically trained psychiatrists would be needed to staff the clinics. A first step, then, would be the expansion of training programs in the early 1920s. Once the training was under way, demonstration clinics focusing on delinquency would be established. The demonstration clinics would serve two purposes: to address the issue of delinquency and to complete the training of psychiatric social workers and new clinicians who would specialize in delinquency. However, the grand design never really happened. For one thing, Healy's work at Chicago demonstrated clearly that psychoanalysis alone had a limited usefulness in dealing with delinquency, and for another, it was difficult to identify a target population if the prevention of delinquency was the purpose. In spite of these difficulties, the clinic idea caught on, and by 1933, the 8 original demonstration clinics expanded to 42. As the number of clinics grew, however, their purpose shifted. The clinics now sought to deal with "problem children"—those children who had emotional problems the clinic might address.[29]

Another reason the clinics turned away from delinquency was that Sheldon and Eleanor Glueck's famous study *One Thousand Delinquents* (1934) found that 88 percent of the boys in the study continued delinquency after their initial involvement with the juvenile court and its associated agencies and programs. Clearly whatever the court was doing was not reducing juvenile recidivism. Healy had warned his readers 15 years before that there were no easy answers. The clinics agreed and shifted their focus to problem children.[30]

The psychological approach to juvenile delinquency also suggested that the problem lay with the individual and not with a variety of social influences. The Gluecks' study seemed to indicate that there were other factors, and the Chicago Area Project, launched in 1934, operated on the theory that much of the behavior of young people was a reasonable response to their surroundings. The Chicago Area Project used a community action approach to delinquency

prevention and tried to resolve issues involving young people at the neighborhood level instead of relying on the police and the courts. Not surprisingly,
there was considerable hostility from the police and social workers to this
approach, even though the project continued until after World War II.[31]

As the full force of the depression swept across the country, social agencies were also hit very hard. As business investment declined precipitously,
people lost their jobs, and production and demand entered a long downward
spiral. As business slowed, tax revenues and contributions to social agencies
also declined.[32]

One reason the budgets and resources of the social agencies dried up so
rapidly was that Herbert Hoover's philosophy of volunteerism meant that
these agencies would be the only ones giving any aid, a kind of "drain the
local agencies first" approach. It was not until the depression deepened that it
became obvious that there were no quick solutions to the serious dislocations
in the American (and the world) economy. Many private social agencies were
forced to cut back dramatically, and some agencies had to cease providing services completely. Staff were laid off, budgets were slashed, and services were
curtailed or canceled. State agencies underwent similar difficulties, but they
did not totally disappear because states could provide resources when private
agencies could not obtain funds.

The Detroit YMCA cut its budget by 66 percent in 1932 and trimmed its
staff by over 50 percent. At the same time, job inquiries from young men
increased dramatically. Over 15,000 sought work, but only 1,100 jobs could
be found. The St. Antoine Branch annual report noted, "this branch presents
one of our most serious problems as far as the branches are concerned, for
while it is a community center for the negro [sic] group, its paying membership including both men and boys is now only 279, which raises the question
if we are to continue this particular phase of our work. How shall we finance
it?" Among the suggestions for the future were reducing the costs of member-
ships (and the level of services) so that more young men could join, and creating a guidance clinic "providing more advice on personal matters as they
relate to hygiene, morals, religion, law and vocations." Leaders of the Y also
suggested a health service.[33]

In 1933 the Y reported that the summer-long camp for privileged boys
had enjoyed increased enrollment, and the demand for lodgings and other
services had nearly overwhelmed the agency, even though it received some
assistance from the Federal Emergency Relief Administration. In the following year, the Y commented at length about "homeless and transient boys"
who had come to their attention:

When we touch the life of these boys and listen to their stories and note the per-
fect willingness to be supported, rather than use their own initiative, it certainly
gives us reason to pause and wonder what the future holds in store for these and

thousands of other boys and girls for whom little constructive work is being done. Certainly no organization can be blind and deaf to changing social conditions and the need of necessary adjustments.

This sort of blaming of young victims was unusual, although the older unemployed came in for similar sorts of criticism. Perhaps it only represented the frustration many staffers in social agencies felt at their own impotence in the face of so much human misery. On the positive side, the report claimed that "according to juvenile court officials, juvenile delinquency has been greatly reduced in communities contiguous to Y.M.C.A. buildings."[34]

By 1937 the Y had apparently solved the problem of drifters. The Y found some jobs for men from Detroit through its vocational division, but there were few out-of-towners among the applicants. "It would seem," the report indicated, "that young men are quite properly being advised to stay at home while the unsettled business situation continues." Two years later, the gloom of the early years of the depression had vanished. Annual reports were once again printed on slick paper (instead of being mimeographed), and most talked about accomplishments and achievements—even at the St. Antoine Branch, where a photograph showing a group of African-American children was captioned: "This mixed group at St. ANTOINE is most active in the entire social and religious life of their community. . . . Here they are going over plans for bringing Christmas cheer to 200 under-privileged boys and girls." And they were also proud of "Another activity of exceptional promise," which was "the recent organization of the First Indian Tribe, a father-and-son program designed primarily to encourage the fathers to assume their natural place of leadership in the guidance, counselling and play of their sons. The meetings are held in homes, each tribe is restricted to 9 fathers and their sons, boys between the ages of 7 and 11."

By 1940 the outbreak of World War II dominated, and the report noted that "blackouts ushered in with the start of the world's sickening conflict have spread from one land to another until some are beginning to wonder if it forebodes a veritable blackout of civilization. But despite this lowering blackness, the YMCA continues to hold high the guiding light of world brotherhood to suffering and bewildered humanity." They also made it policy to open their doors to servicemen, adding that "special regulations have been put into effect making our physical and social facilities available to every man in uniform who is serving with the nation's armed forces."[35]

In the 1920s, various child-helping agencies (including both orphanages and placement agencies) combined to form the Child Welfare League of America. The agencies were especially hard hit as a result of the depression and because they seemed to fall outside the limits of various New Deal programs. In January 1936 C. C. Carsten, the league's executive director, wrote to William J. Norton, secretary of the Michigan Children's Fund, a logical choice because the Michigan Children's Fund had money when many other social agencies did not. Carsten wrote, he said, on behalf of "children very largely lost sight of in recent years—due to the emphasis that has been placed on relief." There were a number of such cases, which included "orphans, half-orphans, children whose lives in their own homes were endangered by improper guardianship, intemperance, and other causes." Carsten went on to explain the current situation with the league. There were 160 member agencies, and all of them had reduced staff and services as a consequence of the depression. For example, "from 1930 to 1933, there was an actual shrinkage of 16,055 in the number of children in care in thirty-two states." This cutback did not represent an improvement, though:

> If one could think that these were all returned to happy and successful homes, it would be a cause for thanksgiving. Unfortunately this is not the case. Many of our member agencies and others have repeatedly notified us that shortage of funds has forced them either to close their doors or discharge children who ought to remain in care.

Carsten went on to explain why "federal funds for relief of the unemployed supported great numbers of children living with their families but could never be used for children out of their own homes, or for those whom it would have been wise to remove from unfit homes." Aid to Dependent Children, the new program under Social Security, did not apply to children in institutional care. What the league wanted was not money to provide service to children but rather $100,000 to restore lost staff. The league members were not concerned about the ultimate fate of children because it was their "conviction that the welfare of these children is close enough to the concern of local government bodies and especially to philanthropic people so that a movement in their behalf will enlist adequate support."[36]

While the Child Welfare League was seeking money to restore staff, other agencies struggled to stay alive. In Pennsylvania, according to the chief of the child welfare division, "because of the continued depression, child welfare services and standards are threatened at many points in both state and local fields. One of the most important activities of the Division last year was its active participation in the defense of the state Department of Welfare against ruthless and destructive 'economy measures.' "[37] Meanwhile, the Home Economics Committee of the Family Service Association of Cleveland was reduced to giving advice on diet and nutrition, as the committee lacked funds for any services, except some limited distribution of food.[38]

One organization that did well in the 1930s while others were struggling was the Save the Children Federation, created in 1932. It was a private, non-sectarian child welfare organization whose purpose was "to assist communities to develop programs for the health, education, and general welfare of the children of the United States and other lands." In the United States, the federation focused on poor rural areas. During the 1930s, it provided assistance that directly aided more than 20,000 children by helping "to supply 60,000 school desks and other essentials to needy school districts." The agency helped with school lunch programs and arranged for the transportation of thousands of British children to the United States during World War II.[39]

Social agencies were on the mend by the end of the depression, and the various New Deal efforts helped relieve some of the burdens. The most important change the agencies saw over the two decades between the wars was the entry of the federal government into the arena. In the 1920s, the Sheppard-Towner Act for the provision of health care to pregnant women and newborn infants established the precedent for federally funded assistance to children. The Aid to Dependent Children section of Social Security continued in that tradition. One consequence of federal involvement was that state and local agencies became more focused in their efforts, and many, such as the Child Welfare League of America, began the transformation from service provision to advocacy. The services social agencies provided probably never fully met the needs of families and children during the interwar years. Because the level of service declined during the depression, at the end of the decade, services were probably still inadequate for all children, but especially so for African-American children. Thus, from the perspective of social service, it is almost impossible to say whether children were better off at the end of the decade. By some measures (such as the declining infant mortality rate), they were, but by others (such as the lack of services), they were not.

7

Children and Youth in the Great Depression and the New Deal

The social misery resulting from the Great Depression was unprecedented in the nation's history. From 1929 to 1933, the gross national product declined by 29 percent, consumption by 18 percent, construction by 78 percent, and investment by 98 percent. Unemployment rose from 3.2 percent to 24.9 percent. Hardly anyone was unaffected. For most Americans (except for African-Americans and farmers, who had already begun to experience hard times before the great crash in 1929), what made the depression so hard to take was that it came on the heels of a time of great prosperity and expansion that seemed to promise indefinite improvement.[1]

The depression had a lasting effect on the children who experienced it. One woman recalled:

> I remember all of a sudden we had to move. My father lost his job and we moved to a double garage. The landlord didn't charge us rent for seven years. We had a coal stove, and we had to each take turns, the three of us kids, to warm our legs. It was awfully cold when you opened those garage doors. We would sleep with rugs and blankets over the top of us. Dress under the sheets.

Later things improved a bit:

> I was about fourteen when I joined the NYA (National Youth Administration). I used to get paid $12.50 every two weeks. Making footlockers. I gave half to my mother. This was the first time I could buy some clothes.[2]

Families facing hard times could rarely hide the truth from their children. Slim Collier recalled being taken to an auction where the family's house,

Young people watching a Works Progress Administration movie (The River) outdoors, Missouri (1939). (Photograph by Barbara H. Wright, National Youth Administration [NYA]. National Archives Neg. 119-G-219-M.)

farm, and personal possessions were sold off. Everyone came because it was a big event. "It was a hilarious thing for us kids," Collier said. "We got together, there were lots of new kids. Games. . . . Gradually, I was aware slightly of the events." The children overheard the adults talking. Collier remembered "the worry and the relief they expressed. . . . the fascination with catastrophe." At age 14, Collier got a job as an itinerant farm worker, cutting asparagus for 15 cents an hour. Asked why people would work for such low wages, he explained that many of the field workers were desperate town workers. "At that time," he explained, "I didn't realize the exploitation, and the competitiveness of workers."[3]

In a follow-up study to *Middletown*, the Lynds published *Middletown in Transition* in 1937. They found that Middletown schools pulled young people in opposite directions. The schools encouraged young people to think for themselves but also stressed the need for sacrifices and lowered ambitions in order to meet the needs of the community. School officials and teachers seemed to fear for their jobs and were thus reluctant to challenge prevailing ideas. An important dilemma characterized Middletown and American society: everyone could agree that young people had the right to improve themselves and that in young people lay the hope of the future. Still, given the privations of the depression, it was difficult, if not impossible, to find a way to give youth and society the hope they needed, especially because there seemed to be so many prior claims on society's limited resources.[4]

Both progress and decline characterized the 1930s for children. The end of funding for the Sheppard-Towner Act—because of opposition from the American Medical Association—was a major setback for those who saw a federal role in prenatal and infant care. Sheppard-Towner had worked—it had demonstrated that preventative health care could reduce infant (and maternal) mortality rates, but in 1929 Congress was no longer afraid of women voters, and the AMA commanded considerable respect. So the program was out, and the groundbreaking experiment in federally funded health care came to an end. It had, however, set a precedent for large federal social programs, including programs for children in the period after World War II. Although the prenatal preventative program under Sheppard-Towner did not continue, concern for the health of children did not wane. Much of the major legislation of the New Deal, such as Social Security or the Fair Labor Standards Act, had a direct impact on children, and, it could be argued, an indirect impact on their health care prospects. Physicians claimed that they could provide preventative care, and the number of nurses working as direct health care providers thus declined. Whatever physicians claimed, infant mortality rates climbed noticeably during the depression years, and lack of access to health care was one of the factors.

The material circumstances of children, documented in numerous studies, declined dramatically as men and women lost their jobs and everyone made do with less. Children took jobs—such as running errands or selling newspapers—when parents could not find work. Children wore hand-me-down clothes and slept three to a bed, and families crowded together to save on the rent. Rural children, though not employed for wages, worked long hours at difficult and dangerous tasks, their labor being a part of the family's survival strategy. Some rural children whose families owned little or no property suffered intensely as the depression deepened and opportunity left the countryside. Schools suffered as well. In some cases, teachers could not be paid; schools closed or held double sessions and put off maintenance for better times. Other services, such as the clinics established under Sheppard-Towner, disappeared or were curtailed. Diets changed. Children no longer ate as well as they had—nor did pregnant women. People accepted what they had to for housing and clothing. Some lost homes and farms and took up a migrant life.

Even with the numbers at hand, it is difficult to imagine the impact of the Great Depression on Americans' lives. Steel plants operated at 12 percent of capacity. Industrial construction declined from $949 million to $74 million between 1929 and 1932. Unemployment had reached 13 million. Famine and homelessness became commonplace. In some cities, people lived in ramshackle shacks known ironically as "Hoovervilles."[5]

The New Deal, with all its complexity, focused on children and youth in a number of ways. Never a consistent program or philosophy, the New Deal sometimes had contradictory programs, and its leaders certainly had contradictory philosophies. With the exceptions of the Children's Bureau[6] and the National Youth Administration, New Deal agencies did not concern themselves primarily with children, yet many New Deal programs had a profound impact on children's lives. Programs that preserved jobs or gave assistance to families improved the material conditions of children's families and children's lives as well.

Children first became aware of the depression when family fortunes obviously fell. Some families disintegrated, but others drew closer together. As Robin Langston of Hot Springs, Arkansas, recalled, "I knew the Depression had really hit when the electric lights went out."[7]

In *Children of the Depression,* a massive study of the impact of the depression on family life, Glen Elder followed up on a study of 167 preadolescent children in Oakland, California, begun in 1931. Elder wished to know how the loss of income had affected the lives of the children. For example, reduced family circumstances led many children to enter the workforce. These circumstances had a lasting effect as well. According to Elder, "a large number of the study members are convinced that hardship in the depression has made a difference in their financial outlook." In addition, "they tend to use the Depression as an explanation for their behavior." As one young white-collar worker put it, he had come to "realize that money doesn't always come so easy. It makes you just a little conservative in spending money, especially in spending it beyond your means."[8]

The lack of mob violence or massive strikes or other forms of radicalism surprised Europeans. Americans were mostly passive in the face of the great economic disaster and rejected European ideas as well as European tactics. In the election of 1932, for example, the Communists polled only 120,000 votes. The lack of action may have meant that many had sunk into despair. Not only had the economy slowed to a standstill, but the birthrate had also fallen. If there were no workers to tend the machines in the factories and thus no future wage earners, how could the economy possibly recover? Some wondered *if* there would be a future. Schools would stand empty, markets would continue to shrink, and the means to recover might never be available.[9]

Existing local agencies were quickly overwhelmed and out of money; still the clients kept coming and the depression kept getting worse. President Hoover tried to stem the tide through pep talks and conferences with industrialists. Let the first burden fall on profits instead of wages, he told them, but the economic decline was so total that such a distinction was soon meaning-less. Hoover, who had a fine international reputation as a humanitarian, believed that local relief and volunteerism should be the main responses. At first he saw no role for the federal government, but the worsening economic news finally led him to establish the Reconstruction Finance Corporation, a way, he thought, of getting business back on its feet.[10]

Meanwhile, at the local level, things only worsened. Social agencies, both public and private, closed their doors, all funds having been expended and all staff long since laid off. Some agencies kept skeleton staffs and dispensed advice. In Cleveland, Ohio, the Home Economics Committee of the Family Service Association was reduced to giving advice about diets and trying to find food to hand out.[11] Also in Cleveland, the Girl's Bureau (it had begun its institutional life as the Women's Protective Association in 1917; it later became the Youth Service Agency) noted that finding work for young women was becoming very difficult. The staff worried about young women slipping into prostitution and redoubled its efforts when that possibility seemed immi-nent.[12] This agency and others serving young women were particularly con-cerned about homeless girls and worked hard to get the message out that help was available. "Offers to Help Homeless Girls" read the headline in the *Cleveland Press* of January 18, 1933. "No doubt vice conditions are increas-ing among girls," Mrs. Winifred Gaehr of the YMCA said, "but it is not because they are forced to stay out nights. It is because they do not apply for help."[13]

In Detroit city fathers sent delegations around to the fire stations to see how many children had lined up for the food dispensed there. Teachers tried to help the least fortunate of their students, and the Children's Fund of Michigan provided funds so that every child, regardless of means, would have a hot lunch at school. The Children's Fund also gave money to the colored branch of the YMCA and supported YMCA summer camps. Staffers at the YMCAs in Detroit saw their budgets decline as their revenues fell off, and they worried about all the transient youth they saw around them; the staffers condemned these young men because of their laziness and lack of initiative.[14]

In July 1940, A. Winnifred Golley, a registered nurse and superintendent of the Central Michigan Children's Clinic, sifted through her files and sent some representative case descriptions to William J. Norton, executive vice president and secretary of the Michigan Children's Fund. What follows is case 1892:

> Patient, age eight months, was admitted to the Central Michigan Children's Clinic on 3-4-39, with the chief complaint of sweating and coughing for past week. The mother states that the patient has been perspiring markedly since December and was irritable when handled. The patient had not been taking formula well, had been getting some cod liver oil of a preparation of bulk cod liver oil. Had not taken any orange juice the past month. On admission the patient appeared to be an

average nourished, acutely ill, white child. Physical examination found that the mouth hygiene was poor, lips scaled and cracked. Chest revealed scorbutic notching, heart was rapid, the buttocks were excoriated. Examination of the extremities were painful on motion of legs.

Treatment was commenced and the baby seemed content as long as permitted to lie quietly, and when handled cried a great deal. The patient expired ten hours after admission. Post mortem examination was performed and it was found that there were numerous petechiae in the serous surfaces of the body, the ribs definitely hemorrhagic and typically scorbutic in character from gross examination.

Final Diagnosis: Scurvy
                   Secondary anemia
                   Malnutrition
                   Impetigo

No financial arrangement was made for the child. No transportation was given by the Judge of Probate. From the final diagnosis we feel had it had care just a few days earlier, its life need not have been lost.[15]

On April 12, 1933, Fred Johnson, general secretary of the Michigan Children's Aid Society, wrote to Secretary Norton describing a case recently handled by the agency for which Johnson worked:

This child came to our attention through the Florence Crittenton Hospital, Detroit, where she was born. Her mother was unmarried and came from a home so poor in an out [of] state county that it was impossible to return the child to that home. The mother became very ill sometime after the birth of the child and died at the Florence Crittenton Hospital. The child was placed in our care and in spite of considerable illness seems to be making steady improvement.[16]

In 1934 Dr. Icie Macy, a Yale graduate in biochemistry and chief researcher at the Children's Fund Research Laboratory, concluded in her annual report to Norton that "very young and rapidly growing infants may not always be able to take a sufficiently large enough quantity of irradiated evaporated milk to completely protect them against rickets. This was demonstrated by the fact that a few of the babies who received irradiated evaporated milk as the sole source of the antirachitic vitamin D, developed some rickets of a very mild degree."[17]

These two cases and the somewhat startling results of nutritional research demonstrate the impact of the Great Depression and the response of a unique social agency to those conditions. The extension of health services to children who lived in rural parts of Michigan and the nutrition research carried on by the laboratories maintained by the fund were but two of the many activities of the Children's Fund of Michigan. Some of the laboratory research—the testing of evaporated milk—had been funded by the Borden Company. Infants born to poor mothers experienced severe problems because the mothers had not eaten well and their milk was deficient. Human milk substitutes were just

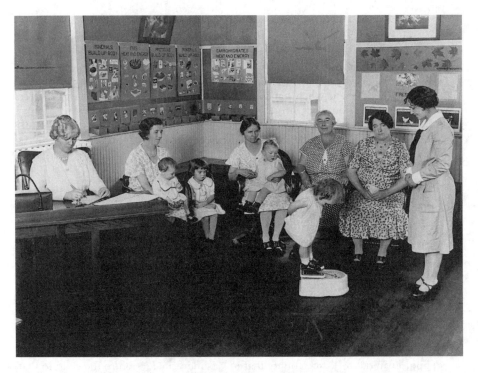

Children's health clinic in a rural school, northern Michigan (ca. 1936). (Photographer unknown. Bentley Historical Library, Ann Arbor, Michigan, Children's Fund Papers, Box 24.)

beginning to appear. Like the distribution of health care, the distribution of adequate nutrition was closely related to income.

The Children's Fund of Michigan was established in 1929 with a gift of $10 million from Senator James Couzens, a Republican who had been one of the founders and an early business manager of the Ford Motor Company. Somewhat unusually, Couzens specified that *all* the money was to be spent within 25 years.[18] Most of the money was spent on child health in rural parts of Michigan, but other funds went to a child guidance clinic in Detroit, Boys Clubs, YMCAs, YWCAs, the Boy Scouts and the Girl Scouts, the Michigan Children's Aid Society (specifically to cover cases such as the one described), the Michigan Children's Village (a Methodist orphanage), a dental clinic in Detroit, summer camps for African-American children and their mothers, and the nutrition research (noted in the foregoing paragraph) that had begun at the Merrill Palmer School in Detroit.[19] The Children's Fund also secretly funded the hot lunch program of the Detroit Public Schools, insisting that students not be able to tell who had paid and who had not. Significantly, the Children's Fund of Michigan had money in the depression when most agencies and public bodies did not.[20]

Because health care was not available in the rural parts of Michigan, some of which were still quite isolated in the 1930s, the Children's Fund set up health districts across the state. The fund sent nurses around the state to do things such as vaccinate against smallpox and diphtheria. They also organized "mothers' classes" and checked children for dental problems. They urged teachers to add instruction in health and nutrition to elementary curricula, and they worked with the county normal schools to put these items in their curricula. One idea that emerged from the early health campaigns in Michigan was a summer camp designed to improve children's health and fitness. The camp at Bay Cliff eventually became a summer retreat for the disabled.[21]

By 1937 the fund had health services of some sort in 53 of 83 rural counties. In that year, Secretary Norton claimed that the program had reduced death rates for both mothers and infants, but he did acknowledge that the infant mortality rate was still higher in the targeted rural counties than for the state as a whole. In the newly created health districts, the fund relied on nurses who were mostly active in health education but also provided some services—especially prenatal care. The fund also sponsored a dental program and an eye program for indigent children. According to Norton, "the work of a nurse is fundamental to the success of all our other health programs. She is a field agent who discovers and gets needy children to medical and dental clinics, who does postnatal and prenatal work in maternity cases, assists in the control of communicable diseases, works at child health inspection, and does many other things."[22]

Some people moved back to the rural countryside during the depression, causing the rural population of Michigan (and that of many other states) to reverse its long-term downward trend briefly in the 1930s. Some rural areas of Michigan, especially the northern part of the lower peninsula and the upper peninsula, suffered extreme deprivation during the depression. These areas had poor soils and short growing seasons, so that the farmers who lived there found that there were no markets for their crops. Children's Fund nurses found no shortage of patients once they got to the rural areas. In July 1930, one of the nurses reported:

> July 8 Mrs Wheeler called for me and we drove to Grayling where we met dr. Howard who took me to Spencer in Kalkaska County to a Preschool Clinic. Spencer was almost inaccessible because of a new roadway being constructed through the sand. We found Miss Hoffa waiting for us in a shack called the church of the Community. The people are seventh Day Adventists, the homes are more unpainted shacks and the country is desolate. However, 17 children with their parents appeared from somewhere. They were clean, thoroughly dressed. The mothers seemed anxious to have them cared for and appreciated the doctor's advice.

The nurses were shocked at the conditions they found in parts of the state, especially in regions where the very poor woodcutters lived. These regions were so remote that they were completely isolated during the winter months.[23]

One difficulty facing the nurses was the reluctance of the probate judges to issue the necessary orders so that children in need of health care could receive it at county expense. Because of the decline in revenues during the depression, the probate judges routinely refused requests for funds. In one instance, the nurses sought action from a probate judge on behalf of a neglected infant being cared for by retarded grandparents. The judge refused, the nurse noting "things were as they were and that was that."[24] Other judges offered rationales for their reluctance, one claiming that hospitals tried to keep patients longer than necessary. Another indicated that he was interested only in children who had some brains. He also objected to a bill of $500 for a crippled child, contending that no child was worth an expenditure that large. Another judge said that he could not provide transportation money for children because the county was building a new courthouse.[25]

Nurses also showed children in rural schools how to test drinking water to ensure that it was safe and in the process called attention to the need for good sanitation practices at the schools. Some rural schools lacked even the dignity of a privy, boys and girls each heading off in different directions to relieve themselves. The visiting nurses provided prenatal care to pregnant women and urged them to visit a doctor. They also taught prenatal classes to groups of pregnant women. The nurses encouraged teachers to promote health education actively and to make home visits in order to identify children in need of medical and dental care. The child health division of the Children's Fund claimed to have had a major impact on the vital statistics of the rural parts of the state. In 1933 the annual report concluded:

> It is a satisfaction to note the lowering infant death rate, the lessening of skin diseases, the fewer absences from the schools because of illness, the increased health consciousness on the part of the teachers and in some localities the noticeable improvement in school sanitation; and above all the growing health consciousness on the part of all the people, and the participation of more and more of local folks in the child health movement, including physicians, as well as school authorities, parents, children, and citizens.[26]

The work of the health service was important and timely during the depression, when infant mortality rates actually went up in the nation as a whole. In many respects, the work of the Children's Fund health service recalled similar efforts around the country under the Sheppard-Towner Act.[27]

From 1932 to 1934, infant mortality rates in the United States rose from 57.6 to 60.1 per 1,000 live births. White rates went from 53.3 to 54.5 in that period, but African-American rates went from 86.2 to 94.4.[28] In Michigan, by contrast, the infant mortality rates went back down, and the Children's Fund undoubtedly deserved some of the credit for that reversal.[29] By the end of the decade, the health service was pulling back from its earlier efforts because they argued that many of the acute problems noted earlier had been addressed. Michigan had enacted a sales tax during the depression, and the tax had brought in enough revenue so that many state services had been at least partially restored by the end of the decade.[30]

During the same period, the fund was also supporting nutritional research under the direction of Dr. Icie Macy at the Children's Fund laboratory. Macy directed the laboratory throughout the 1930s, and her work helped to establish the importance of sound nutrition for infants. One of the primary issues in infant feeding in the 1920s and 1930s was the use of "infant formulas." The basic idea of the formulas was that professionals, relying on science, could develop an infant-feeding substance that would be superior to human milk. The fetish of science was so important that the American Medical Association refused to run advertisements for infant formulas to be administered without prescriptions. Macy's work at the Children's Fund laboratory was at the forefront of the scientific study of infant feeding.

Macy began work on the study of evaporated milk for the Borden Company in 1934. The company wanted to advertise its milk as being equal to, or better than, human milk. As the study proceeded, it became clear that there were some difficulties. The research was done in a fairly standard, if naive, scientific manner: one group received the condensed milk with vitamin D added, and another the milk without the vitamin D. Babies in both groups developed rickets, a nutritional disorder that causes bones to fail to take on enough calcium, owing to a vitamin D deficiency. Macy called in Dr. Martha Eliot of the Federal Children's Bureau, who confirmed Macy's diagnosis of rickets in both groups. The control group had been expected to get rickets, and treatment was quickly and readily provided (rickets is correctable with vitamin D supplements), but the fact that the experimental group also showed signs of the disease was particularly troubling. In the annual report for 1934–1935, Macy concluded:

> Very young and rapidly growing infants may not always be able to take a sufficiently large enough quantity of irradiated evaporated milk to completely protect them against rickets. This was demonstrated by the fact that a few of the babies who received irradiated evaporated milk as the sole source of the antirachitic vitamin D, developed some rickets of a very mild degree. In practically every case where rickets did occur it was healing and definitely under control."[31]

The researchers not only moved quickly to treat the research subjects but also made dietary supplements available to other destitute families.

The situation at the research laboratory was troubling. Not surprisingly, the Borden Company did not want the results of this study published, and Macy consulted her major professor, Dr. Lafayette B. Mendel of Yale, about the situation:

We have felt somewhat concerned over the vitamin D activity of the milk because we have had craniotabes develop right under our eyes. Of course our babies are started on the evaporated milk study any time from the tenth day to the second month of life and the quantity of milk taken is small at this period. Consequently the unitage of Vitamin D is small.

Mendel wrote back immediately, concerned about keeping "a proper brake on the hasty activities of the various evaporated milk companies. Many of them have received licenses and are preparing to market a product containing vitamin D with the *implication* that they are distributing a safe antirachitic."[32]

Despite the desire of the Borden Company to keep the research under wraps and Macy's own reluctance to go public with what she believed were preliminary results, the story of her work got out. Martha Guernsey Colby, a physiological psychologist at the University of Michigan, wrote Macy with disturbing news on May 4, 1936: "Last week at the mid-western meetings of the American Psychological Association, I reported a study of maturation in which the rickets data were used." Colby claimed it was not intentional. "I had strictly not intended to do this without your official consent, but it focused everyone's attention at once, and Prof. [John] Anderson, Chairman of the Child Development Institute at Minnesota, was kind enough to state publicly that even the preliminary study was a 'superlative and brilliant approach to basic problems of body-mind development.' " Colby indicated that she was "surprised and pleased at the reaction to a purely preliminary study." Later, at another meeting, "at least ten people referred to it, and all were emphatic in asking that what data we have, be published at once, strictly stating, of course, its introductory nature."[33]

Macy wrote to L. J. Auerbacher, vice president of the Dry Milk Company, a Borden subsidiary, about the delicate matter of publishing the results, saying pointedly, "I think it would be very unwise not to make our data available in the Journal of Pediatrics with a plea for more careful standardization of methods of clinical study and analysis of data. The paper can be presented in such a way as to fortify the irradiated milk program and not to confuse it."[34]

In December 1934, at the annual meeting of the Society for Research in Child Development, in the discussion following a presentation about calcium metabolism by Amy Daniels of Iowa, Macy's research came up for extensive discussion. Frederick Tisdall of the University of Toronto observed that there was "conclusive evidence that vitamin D is necessary for normal nutrition during the age of infancy," and added, "There is great need for further information on the relative efficiency of different sources of vitamin D and the requirements of this vitamin at different ages." In the discussion that followed, Macy and Dr. Marsh Poole of Children's Hospital in Detroit expanded on their study using irradiated evaporated milk:

The infants were all less than three months with an average age of six weeks at the beginning of the period of observation. Seventy-three were given irradiated evaporated milk from October to May. Rickets developed in a considerable number. This was true, in spite of the fact that the infants were taking more vitamin D in the form of irradiated evaporated milk, as judged by biologic assays on animals, than the minimum amount alleged to be necessary when the same quantity is given in the form of irradiated fresh liquid milk. Even after the irradiated evaporated milk has stood for a period of a year it still shows a biological potency of 50 to 60 international units of vitamin D per quart of reconstructed milk. The incidence of rickets in the group of babies on the irradiated was less than in a similar group of fifty babies on the same evaporated milk base without irradiation. In a like manner the ingestions were less numerous and less severe in the former group. When rickets was noted in the latter group the infants were given a freshly irradiated evaporated milk for an average of twenty-two days. A considerable number showed healing in some degree, others were unchanged. Attention is called to the fact that very small infants, or infants who are partially breast fed, are often unable to take sufficient irradiated evaporated milk to adequately protect them from rickets. Furthermore, the prevention of rickets in very young babies, such as those used in this study, and according to Dr. [Martha] Eliot [of the Federal Children's Bureau] is the most rigorous clinical requirement for testing a vitamin D fortified milk; it is by such a test, however, that a milk to be used for routine prevention of rickets must be judged.[35]

Now the word was out about evaporated milk, but the Borden people could take some comfort from the finding that their milk helped to reduce rickets in the control group. Essentially the difficulty was that very young infants could not get enough vitamin D from evaporated milk. The fundamental problem was conceptual. Researchers working on infant nutrition were guilty of being too simplistic about the way human infants feed, not realizing that a complex biochemical exchange—and not a simple mechanical one— was taking place.[36]

The activities of the fund improved the quality of life for thousands of rural children in Michigan during the depression, but the fund's activities also aided in the development of sound knowledge about how infants take nourishment, an important piece in the puzzle of how to reduce infant mortality. Indeed, it is the infant mortality rate that links these two activities. Access to health care is vital if infant mortality is to be lowered; likewise, sound scientific knowledge of infant nutrition is equally important for infant health. Dr. Macy and others engaged in nutritional research, such as Amy Daniels at the Iowa Child Welfare Research Station, had to develop a more sophisticated approach to the scientific study of infant feeding. Only by understanding the implications of a flawed research design such as that undertaken by Macy and funded by Borden could researchers come to a level of understanding sufficient to have a positive impact on children's health.

During the Great Depression, the Children's Fund of Michigan made health care available to the state's poorest children and also made basic research in human nutrition possible. Thus the fund made important contributions both to children in the 1930s and to generations of children who benefited from the nutritional research performed at the Children's Fund Research Laboratories. But not all local agencies were so lucky. In fact, most were forced to reduce or eliminate both staff and services, and some agencies, such as orphanages, were overwhelmed with new clients. And in most states, the infant mortality rates increased during this period, an incontrovertible sign that the depression was bad for children. The children of Michigan were lucky; children in other states were not.

The New Deal

The New Deal was really a hodgepodge of conflicting programs and ideas. It was a series of specific responses to specific problems or issues. Underneath all the overlap and confusion, however, the Roosevelt administration was consistent about both its approach to problems and the kinds of problems it addressed. There was a basic distrust of financial experts, a reliance on centralized planning such as had occurred during the Great War, and a strong focus on social problems, in part because so many important members of the Roosevelt administration had been either social workers or settlement house residents.

The New Deal began with the famous "hundred days" of the first three months of Roosevelt's first term. The specific acts of legislation are less important than the change in mood and spirit that flowed from the new administration's emphasis on action. Congress moved quickly to deal with a bank crisis, then to placate angry farmers, and then to develop programs for the unemployed and to protect home owners. But it was also becoming clear that the federal government would have to undertake the enormous task of providing emergency relief to families and individuals who were out of work or who had lost everything in bank failures. This was precisely the step that Herbert Hoover had resisted for so long. To deal with the banks, Congress created the Federal Emergency Relief Administration in May 1933. Soon afterward Congress established the Civil Works Administration (CWA) to provide jobs for the unemployed. Plagued by poor administration and a lack of planning, the CWA quickly developed a reputation for make-work and boondoggling. Some taint from the CWA probably affected the Works Progress Administration (WPA), created in 1935, but it became the federal government's largest and most important relief effort.[37]

Children and young men benefited directly from two federal efforts: the Civilian Conservation Corps (CCC) and the National Youth Administration

Boys outside NYA training center, Detroit, Michigan (ca. 1938). (Photographer unknown, NYA. National Archives Neg. 119-G-3408-D.)

(NYA). Young men joined the CCC and then worked on various conservation and civic projects around the country, the idea being that they could do useful things that might otherwise not get done and earn a little money (they were required to send a certain amount home each month). The NYA was supposed to help young people of high school and college age stay in school by setting up work-study programs through which they could earn some money.

Preparing free lunches for NYA youth, Washington, D.C. (ca. 1938). (Photograph by Dan Nichols, NYA. National Archives Neg. 119-G-4109-D.)

At the same time, the program would help save the jobs of teachers at both the high school and college levels.

Many young men avoided the CCC because of the military character of its organization; there was nothing like the CCC for young women. To meet the growing needs of young people, Roosevelt created the NYA by executive order in 1935. It administered four different types of programs for youth aged 16 to 25. There was work-study for students from families on relief, employment on work projects for those out of school, vocational assistance, and organized recreation. Over 2.5 million young people were involved in the work projects during the years of the NYA (it lasted until 1943). The NYA tried to serve equal numbers of male and female youth, but it did little to challenge prevailing gender role stereotypes. Thus young men were more likely to obtain marketable skills, whereas young women received training in home economics. Both the CCC and the NYA included African-Americans in their programs, but the agencies did little to confront prevailing racial prejudice.[38]

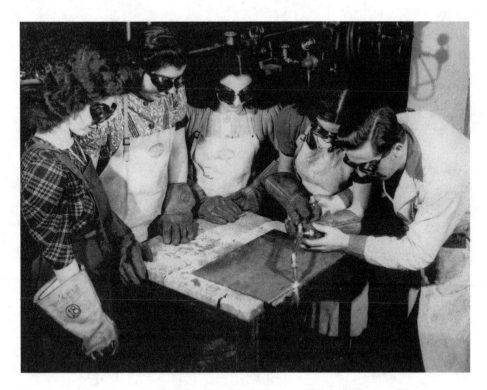

Girls in a welding shop, Queens, New York (1940). Over 3,000 young men and women were training at the Astoria Training Center in auto repair, sheet metal work, furniture repair, upholstery, welding, sewing, and painting. (Photograph by Harold Corsini, NYA. National Archives Neg. 119-S-20G-2.)

In 1939 the NYA began teaching industrial skills related to defense work to males. As the draft depleted the ranks of young men, NYA officials extended industrial training to young women in 1940. Although some young women learned industrial skills, the NYA continued to emphasize domestic images in its promotional material and thus may have contributed to the expectation that Rosie would go back home after the war was over.

Despite obvious biases, the NYA dealt more directly with the issue of race than many other federal agencies during the New Deal years because Mary McLeod Bethune, the founder of Bethune-Cookman College in Daytona Beach, Florida, was a member of the advisory committee for the NYA. Mrs. Bethune worked to ensure that young black people received the same services through the NYA as did young white people.[39]

In her 1938 report for the Division of Negro Affairs, Mrs. Bethune praised what had been accomplished but also pointed out many deficiencies,

NYA machine shop. Girls working on a metal lathe (ca. 1938). (Photograph by Barbara H. Wright, NYA. National Archives Neg. 119-3621-D.)

noting in particular that young black people did not have equal access to the more desirable programs such as apprenticeship training or the vocational guidance program. She called for a number of improvements, including the idea that the NYA "foster and gain the cooperation of the WPA for the setting up of a curative mecca for crippled Negro children similar to the nationally famous Warm Springs Foundation from which Negroes are barred."[40]

From 1935 to 1943, the NYA aided over 600,000 college-aged youth and over 1.5 million high school aged young people through its work-study programs. It also provided skills training and led to the construction or establishment of over 3,000 educational buildings.[41]

Even more far-reaching than the NYA, especially in terms of affecting the lives of children, was Social Security. Roosevelt proposed Social Security in January 1935. The idea behind this legislation was to create a national system to remedy some of the defects of existing relief programs. There was little disagreement over the idea for a national system of old-age and survivors' insurance, but the question of unemployment compensation proved much more difficult. Because it was housed in the Department of Labor, the Chil-

Girls in welding training outside training center, Detroit, Michigan (ca. 1938). (Photographer unknown, NYA. National Archives Neg. 119-G-3627-D.)

dren's Bureau was invited to submit papers pertaining to the proposed Social Security law.[42]

The Children's Bureau study "Security for Children" was a brief for basic economic security for children, especially the right to adequate conditions in which to grow. Lenroot and Eliot contended that

Security for families, the broad foundation upon which the welfare of American children must rest, involves economic, health, and social measures which pertain to the entire economic and social structure of our civilization. Among them are an adequate wage level and a reasonable workday and workweek, with provision of regular and full employment necessary to yield a stable and sufficient family income; unemployment insurance or compensation when full employment fails; provision of adequate medical care and promotion of physical and mental health.

They argued that all Social Security measures were in reality child welfare measures. Old-age pensions, for example, relieved families with children at home of the burden of caring for aged parents. The need for Social Security came also from the shocking realization that 40 percent of the people on relief were children under age 16—a total of 8 million.[43]

Meanwhile, in passing the Social Security Act of 1935, the federal government had begun the principal system of social welfare in the United States. In comparison with social welfare in other industrialized countries, the system established by Social Security was conservative and the benefits low. Many classes of workers, such as domestics and agricultural laborers, were not covered, and many of the causes of poverty, such as sickness and disability, were not adequately addressed. Yet the Social Security Act was a major turning point in American history. The payment of Social Security taxes gave most working Americans an unassailable claim to Social Security benefits.[44]

At the same time, the Social Security Act established a federal presence in social welfare and inaugurated federal aid to children. At first called Aid to Dependent Children and later Aid to Families of Dependent Children (AFDC), the federal welfare system arose out of the concerns expressed by the Children's Bureau staff report. The system was administered by states according to national guidelines. Although this section of the Social Security Act established precedent for the right to aid for dependent children, aiding children was not the primary focus of Social Security legislation, and Congress was relatively uninterested in the provisions pertaining to children. Aid to dependent children was an outgrowth of efforts begun early in the century to aid desperate mothers and enable them to keep their children. Most of the states had established mother's aid laws by 1931, but as historian Leroy Ashby observes, "the programs tended to be permissive rather than mandatory, minuscule in coverage, and at the mercy of local politics." Although the system seemed to establish a right to support, those rights were contingent upon the favors of local officials. Thus the system in effect reduced mothers to the status of beggars and may well have harmed the interests of children supposedly being protected.[45]

Title V of the Social Security Act provided federal grants-in-aid to states for the expansion of services for neglected and abused children, but in some cases little or nothing was done. The Federal Emergency Relief Association had provided much direct assistance to children (shoes and clothing, for example), but in other states, there was a delay in creating the program. In Mississippi, for example, no ADC program was established until 1941.[46]

Other New Deal agencies also assisted children. The WPA established nursery schools staffed by unemployed teachers. The FERA and later the WPA provided housekeeping aid to families that had children or dependent elderly people in the home. The program was designed not only to help the needy families but also to provide employment to the aides.[47]

Of all the aid programs for children in the 1930s, day nurseries probably aroused the most public interest and support. Many middle-class families used these schools as day care centers, thus establishing a kind of precedent for federally funded day care centers and breaking the old notion that day care was for poor or pathological families only. The need for such services had been made real by the circumstances of the depression, but nursery schools proved so popular that many families urged their continuation even as economic services improved.[48] In its final report, the WPA claimed that nursery schools had not only improved the lives of children because of the medical care provided and the healthful environment, including nutritious meals, but also gave employment to teachers, nurses, dietitians, and other workers.[49]

Conclusion

If the Great Depression was a profound shock to the American system, the New Deal was an unprecedented response to the circumstances of the depression. From the vantage point of children and youth in American society, New Deal programs looked like a continuation of the programs pioneered by the Children's Bureau in the 1920s. The New Deal may have established many precedents for government intervention in the lives of ordinary Americans, but the idea that the government could assist children, improve the quality of their lives, and thereby promote the future health and welfare of the nation can be traced to the Sheppard-Towner Act, if not further back. Had it not been for the pioneering efforts of the Children's Bureau, the shape of New Deal legislation could have been substantially altered, and the assistance rendered to American children during the 1930s substantially lessened.

The files of social agencies and the work of organizations such as the Michigan Children's Fund demonstrate the range and depth of the impact of the depression. They show that the nation was in the grip of a social disaster of unprecedented magnitude. Starvation threatened many Americans, and as adults suffered, so children did too. Children born in the worst years of the depression may have been irreversibly harmed by the poor diets forced upon their mothers. Many children's illnesses and crippling conditions went untreated for lack of resources. Some children even died because no one could provide the medical care needed.

The nation responded, though reluctantly, to the challenges economic stagnation presented. Young men were the chief benefactors. One agency, the CCC, was designed exclusively for them, and another, the NYA, also directed much of its efforts into keeping young men in school and preparing for a better future. Young women, whose presence in the workforce increased in spite of the hard times, benefited from the NYA but had to be content with gender stereotypes that denied young women the same bright economic future envisioned for young men. Ironically, because of the outbreak of World War II, it was young women who swelled the ranks of industry as the depression ended; young men went to war.

Did the programs for children and the efforts of the Children's Bureau mean that the nation had become more committed to the welfare of its children? The subsequent history of the welfare provisions of Social Security (ADC—later AFDC) suggests that the record was at best mixed. More children in indigent homes did benefit from an expanded welfare system, but that system proved to be less than effective in giving children the kind of economic support they needed to escape the welfare dependence of their parents. At the same time, infant mortality rates declined, and child health improved, so that more children lived longer and suffered less from debilitating illnesses. The tremendous expansion of the birthrate after World War II clearly established the optimism of Americans after the war and their belief in, and concern for, their children.

The history of the depression shows that children suffer at least as much as adults from hard times and economic deprivation. The New Deal demonstrated that government can respond to human misery and can at the same time develop programs designed to benefit children and youth and thereby invest in the future of society. Programs such as Sheppard-Towner suggest that a residual concern for the welfare of children has probably always existed in American society and that even in a conservative age, the efforts of child advocates can sometimes succeed and children can benefit. On the whole, however, it must be noted that the United States is not an especially child-friendly society. Despite impressive economic achievements, much of that success has come at the expense of a great deal of human misery, much of it the misery of children who suffer through no fault of their own.

8

Conclusion

Superficially no two decades in American history seem more different than the two between the great global wars of the twentieth century. The 1920s were a time of growth and prosperity; a time of "flaming youth," of expanded amusements and awareness of national themes; a time of movies and heroes, of Babe Ruth and Charles Lindbergh. All this wonderful growth came crashing down in the Great Depression of the 1930s, and although the federal government's role in society and the economy expanded in an unprecedented way, the American people were permanently scarred by the experience of hard times—or so it seemed at a glance and at a distance.

Regarding American children and youth, the theme of expansion and contraction for the two decades can certainly be maintained. Children and youth in the 1920s gained greater control over their own lives and spaces as they formed peer groups and found ways to adjust to the realities of urban life, compulsory school attendance, city jobs, or college attendance. The novelty of the city, the unlimited possibilities the future seemed to hold, and the end of old constraints and social customs combined to make the 1920s a golden age of youth, a good time to be young and optimistic. By contrast, the 1930s represented major contractions, a loss of innocence and possibility, the dwindling of opportunities and a growing sense of foreboding, a time when sacrifice, rather than optimism, seemed to be the essential value to teach young people.

In the 1920s, everything seemed possible. Young women could combine marriage and a career, and child experts could provide the advice needed to make it all work. By the 1930s, young women had to abandon elaborate dreams of freedom and expanded roles. Some stayed home to contribute to the family economy through domestic work; others took menial jobs to add their meager income to the family resources; and most had to postpone or abandon efforts to get married because young men, desperate for work, had to give up any idea of settling down to family life because they lacked the means to support a family.

Young children faced similar difficulties. Finding work—even the most menial sorts of work—meant that they, too, could contribute to the family economy. Many things had to be given up: new clothes, toys, games, amusements. In the 1920s, when young children had money, they spent it; in the 1930s, they brought it home to help with the basic necessities of family life. Some children and youth left school and home to find work. Some stayed home because they had no money to spend. All shared in the declining fortunes of their families. Some even suffered and died because of the lack of money for health care.

To see the period in terms of contrasts is not wrong, but to focus only on those contrasts is to ignore many other trends and developments that not only continued from the 1920s to the 1930s but also expanded during the latter decade. Many such developments, such as the rise of child science, have continued to have a major impact on American society throughout the twentieth century. The increase of information about children—what historian Hamilton Cravens has called "the science of the normal child"—continued throughout the 1920s and the 1930s. By 1940 child experts knew a great deal more about how children grew, what their nutritional requirements were, how they developed intellectually and psychologically, and how to prevent many of the diseases and misfortunes of children. Although some children died because of conditions during the depression, others born decades later in some cases lived longer and better lives because of the research child scientists conducted in the 1930s.

Even if the 1930s represented a contraction of opportunities for young people, many developments of the 1920s remained. Peer groups continued to provide a major part of the socialization for children and youth. Dating and petting, novelties much discussed in the popular press in the 1920s, became commonplace and thus unremarked in the 1930s. If young women saw the idea of combining marriage and a career fade in the 1930s, many young married women did just that—they worked when their husbands could not and in many cases kept the family afloat economically. Other young women worked to support themselves and their families.

Government trends went the opposite way of economic and social trends—the federal government became more active and more present in the lives of Americans after the beginnings of the New Deal. Certainly, compared with the philosophy of the Coolidge and Hoover administrations this was true, but viewed from a child's eye, this generalization must be modified. The Federal Children's Bureau, from its inception, had always been in close, even personal, touch with ordinary Americans. And the bureau pioneered in federal legislation designed to remedy social ills and improve the lives of American children. A federal law to ban child labor was one of the bureau's early efforts; Sheppard-Towner was another. These efforts began well before the 1930s—it was during the 1930s that the goals laid down much earlier finally were achieved. Only when the nation was in dire distress did the needs of children receive adequate support at the federal level.

When World War II blazed forth in Europe, American society had been profoundly transformed by the experiences of the 1920s and 1930s. A modern industrial, urban, and metropolitan culture had emerged. Small-town America had retreated to the margins. Cities housed the bulk of the American population, and in cities, American children learned how to take control of a part of their own lives, to find ways to adjust to the realities of compulsory school attendance and to the conformities metropolitan America sought to impose on its future citizens. The depression had sobered Americans and had rendered the children who grew up under its influence permanently conservative about financial matters. Yet much of what had been laid down in these two decades—compulsory school attendance laws, laws against child labor, studies in child science and health, nursery schools and parent education, to name some—endured.

Chronology

1899   Illinois creates the first Juvenile Court.

1909   First White House Conference on Children.

1911   Illinois passes the first Mothers' Pension Law.

1912   United States Children's Bureau established.

1915   Cleveland Conference on American Schools begins.

1914   Sommerville, Massachusetts, creates a prototype for junior high schools.

1916   Keating Owen Act prohibiting child labor passed.

1917   Iowa Child Welfare Research Station established. Women's Protective Association established in Cleveland, Ohio.

1918   *Hammer v. Dagenhart* Supreme Court case declares the Keating Owen Act unconstitutional. Laura Spelman Rockefeller Memorial, which would be instrumental in supporting the growth of child development research, founded.

1919   Second White House Conference on Children focuses on child welfare and calls for universally available health care.

1920   U.S. Census indicates that more Americans live in urban than in rural areas. Average daily school attendance reaches 16 million. Commonwealth Fund (established in 1918) decides to focus on the problem of Juvenile Delinquency and set up Child Guidance Clinics. Infant mortality rate in the United States is approximately 100 per 1,000 live births. Child Welfare League of America formed.

1921   Sheppard-Towner Act passed. This act creates a federal-state joint program to provide prenatal care and education designed to reduce infant mortality.

1922   Congress, with the support of the Children's Bureau and orga-
        nized labor, recommends a federal anti–child labor amend-
        ment, which is strongly opposed by factory owners and many
        others, including farmers. The PTA in Port Huron, Michigan,
        hears criticism of the new youthful custom of dating. Lewis
        Terman publishes *Intelligence Tests and School Reorganization,*
        a work that advocates ability tracking in the schools. Iowa
        Child Welfare Research Station establishes the first research
        nursery school.

1923   American Child Health Association founded.

1924   American Orthopsychiatric Association established.

1925   Aided by a grant from the Laura Spelman Rockefeller Memor-
        ial, Cornell University establishes child study clubs. President
        Calvin Coolidge commends the YMCA for providing "training
        for citizenship."

1927   *Child Development Abstracts* begins publication.

1928   Merriam Report, sponsored by "Red Progressives" (reformers
        who were concerned about Native Americans), finds conditions
        on Indian reservations and in boarding schools deplorable.
        John B. Watson publishes *Psychological Care of the Infant and
        Child.* Children's Aid Society of Cleveland changes its focus
        from orphans to dependent, neglected, and abused children.

1929   The programs established under the Sheppard-Towner Act come
        to an end because of active opposition from the American Med-
        ical Association. Senator James Couzzens of Michigan gives $10
        million to establish the Children's Fund of Michigan.

1930   Average daily school attendance reaches 21 million. Infant mor-
        tality in the United States is approximately 69 per 1,000 live
        births. White House Conference on Child Health and Protec-
        tion.

1931   Florence Goodenough and John Anderson publish *Experimen-
        tal Child Study.*

1932   Save the Children Federation created.

1933   Under the National Recovery Administration, codes prohibiting
        child labor are passed. (The NRA is declared unconstitutional
        in 1935.) Civilian Conservation Corps (CCC) established, pro-
        viding jobs for unmarried young men aged 17 to 33.

1934   The Federal Children's Bureau prepares a staff study, "Security
        for Children," which later becomes the basis for the Aid to
        Dependent Children (ADC) part of Social Security. Congress
        passes the Wheeler-Howard Act (Indian New Deal), which
        restores tribal government and some rights to Native American

families (children no longer forcibly sent to boarding school). Society for Research in Child Development established. Sheldon and Eleanor Glueck publish *One Thousand Delinquents.* Chicago Area Project to reduce juvenile delinquency through prevention launched.

1935   Congress passes the Social Security Act, which includes programs for grants-in-aid to states for Aid to Dependent Children (ADC), maternal and child health programs, crippled children's programs, and child welfare services. National Youth Administration established to employ students and needy youth aged 16 to 25. In *Schecter Poultry Corporation v. United States,* the Supreme Court declares the National Industrial Recovery Act, and with it the National Recovery Administration, unconstitutional. Child labor is again legal.

1938   Congress passes the Fair Labor Standards Act, the first permanent federal anti–child labor law. New York City establishes the Standing Committee on Negro Welfare.

1939   At the National Association for Nursery Education annual meeting, psychologist Jean Macfarlane reports that children's IQs can be improved.

1940   White House Conference on Children in a Democracy is concerned about inequities among children and about the rising threat of fascism. Davis and Dollard publish *Children of Bondage,* a study of African-American youth in the American South. Average daily school attendance is 22 million.

1941   In *U.S. v. Darby,* the Supreme Court holds the child labor provisions of the Fair Labor Standards Act constitutional.

Notes

Preface

1. Joseph M. Hawes, *Children in Urban Society: Juvenile Delinquency in the Nineteenth Century* (New York: Oxford University Press, 1971).
2. Hamilton Cravens, *Before Head Start: The Iowa Station and America's Children* (Chapel Hill and London: University Press of North Carolina, 1993); Kristie Lindenmeyer, *"A Right to Childhood": The U.S. Children's Bureau and Child Welfare, 1912–1946* (Urbana: University of Illinois Press, 1997); Richard Reiman, *The New Deal and American Youth: Ideas and Ideals in a Depression Decade* (Athens: University of Georgia Press, 1992).

Chapter 1

1. For a comprehensive account of the rise of child science, see Hamilton Cravens, *Before Head Start: The Iowa Station and America's Children* (Chapel Hill and London: University Press of North Carolina, 1993). For comprehensive guides to the literature on children and childhood in the United States, see Joseph M. Hawes and N. Ray Hiner, *American Childhood: A Research Guide and Historical Handbook* (Westport, Conn., and London: Greenwood Press, 1985); N. Ray Hiner and Joseph Hawes, *Growing Up in America* (Urbana: University of Illinois Press, 1985); and Robert Bremner et al., eds., *Children and Youth in America: A Documentary History* (Cambridge: Harvard University Press, 1970–1974). For a broader historical view of childhood, see Joseph M. Hawes and N. Ray Hiner, *Children in Historical and Comparative Perspective* (Westport, Conn., and London: Greenwood Press, 1991). See also Elliott West and Paula Petrik, eds., *Small Worlds: Children and Adolescents in America, 1850–1950* (Lawrence: University Press of Kansas, 1992); and Harvey J. Graff, *Conflicting Paths: Growing*

Up in America (Cambridge, Mass., and London: Harvard University Press, 1995).

2. Cravens, *Before Head Start,* 99–100; Nancy Bayley, interview with Milton J. E. Senn, 30 October 1969, Child Development Interviews, National Library of Medicine. Many women in psychology were employed in the three long-term longitudinal studies at the Institute of Child Welfare at the University of California–Berkeley. The Guidance Study, under Jean W. Macfarlane, sought to test the usefulness of "intensive and extensive discussion with parents about child-training procedures, family member personality characteristics, interpersonal relationships, health, background, social status, and so forth." The second, the Berkeley Growth Study, under Nancy Bayley and Lotta V. Wolff, was "designed as an intensive investigation of physical, mental, physiological, and motor development in the first 15 months of postpartum life." The third study, begun as the Adolescent Growth Study and renamed the Oakland Growth Study, under Harold E. Jones and Herbert R. Stolz, was designed to "investigate adolescent growth and change in a wide number of aspects." From Mary Cover Jones et al., eds., *The Course of Human Development: Selected Papers from the Longitudinal Studies, Institute of Human Development, the University of California, Berkeley* (Waltham, Mass.: Xerox College Publishing, 1971), 3–4.

3. The two premier peer group studies are Paula Fass, *The Damned and the Beautiful: American Youth in the 1920s* (New York: Oxford University Press, 1977) for college-aged peer groups; and David Nasaw, *Children of the City at Work and at Play* (Garden City, N.Y.: Anchor/Doubleday, 1985) for younger children and city streets.

4. There is a voluminous literature about child labor. See, for example, Joseph M. Hawes, *The Children's Rights Movement: A History of Advocacy and Protection* (Boston: Twayne, 1991), chap. 4. The standard account of the national expansion of education is Lawrence Cremin, *American Education: The Metropolitan Experience* (New York: Harper and Row, 1988).

5. See David Nasaw, *Going Out: The Rise and Fall of Public Amusements* (New York: Basic Books, 1993) for a discussion of the rise and social importance of motion pictures during the period.

6. For a discussion of family life in the 1920s, see Steven Mintz and Susan Kellogg, *Domestic Revolutions: A Social History of American Family Life* (New York: Free Press, 1988).

7. Fass is especially helpful on the matter of changing mores among older middle-class young people, but see also Elizabeth Ewen, *Immigrant Women in the Land of Dollars: Life and Culture on the Lower East Side, 1890–1925* (New York: Monthly Review Press, 1985) and John Modell, *Into One's Own: From Youth to Adulthood in the United States,*

1920–1975 (Berkeley: University of California Press, 1989) for further discussion.

8. The best treatment of the Federal Children's Bureau is the study by Kristie Lindenmeyer, *A Right to Childhood: The U.S. Children's Bureau and Child Welfare, 1912–1946,* (Urbana: University of Illinois Press, 1997). See also Sonya Michel, "Children's Interests/ Mother's Rights: Women, Professionals, and the American Family, 1920–1945" (Ph.D. diss., Brown University, 1986), 114.

9. In addition to Cravens, *Before Head Start,* and Michel, "Children's Interests/Mother's Rights," see also Margo Horn, *Before It's Too Late: The Child Guidance Movement in the United States, 1922–1945* (Philadelphia: Temple University Press, 1989) for a comprehensive treatment of the child guidance movement.

10. For an introduction to the discussion of the motives of social scientists (a vast and not fully explored terrain), see Carl Degler, *In Search of Human Nature: The Decline and Revival of Darwinism in American Social Thought* (New York: Oxford University Press, 1991).

11. A broad treatment of women's issues in the period can be found in Sheila Rothman, *Woman's Proper Place: A History of Changing Ideology and Practice, 1870 to the Present* (New York: Basic Books, 1978); but see also Nancy Cott, *The Grounding of Modern Feminism* (New Haven: Yale University Press, 1987) and Molly Ladd-Taylor, *Women, Child Welfare, and the State* (Urbana: University of Illinois Press, 1994).

12. The standard history of African-Americans in American life is John Hope Franklin and Alfred A. Moss Jr., *From Slavery to Freedom: A History of African-Americans* (New York: McGraw-Hill, 1994). See also Harvard Sitkof, *The Depression Decade,* vol. 1 of *A New Deal for Blacks: The Emergence of Civil Rights as a National Issue* (New York: Oxford University Press, 1978).

Chapter 2

1. Social Science Research Council, *The Statistical History of the United States from Colonial Times to the Present* (Stamford, Conn.: Fairfield Publishers, 1967), 9, table A 34–50. In 1920 the total urban population was 54 million, whereas the total nonurban population was 52 million.

2. Joseph Kett, *Rites of Passage: Adolescence in America, 1790 to the Present* (New York: Basic Books, 1977), 21.

3. See, for example, Jane Jacobs, *The Economy of Cities* (New York: Vintage Books, 1970) and David Nasaw, *Children of the City at Work and at Play* (Garden City, N.Y.: Anchor/Doubleday, 1985).

4. Nasaw, *Children,* 20.

5. Christine Stansell, *City of Women: Sex and Class in New York, 1789–1860* (Urbana: University of Illinois Press, 1987), 209–14.

6. Nasaw, *Children,* 27.

7. For an account of the early history of the juvenile court, see Joseph M. Hawes, *Children in Urban Society: Juvenile Delinquency in the Nineteenth Century* (New York: Oxford University Press, 1971), chap. 11 and 12.

8. William A. Healy, *The Individual Delinquent: A Textbook of Diagnosis and Prognosis for All Concerned in Understanding Offenders* (Boston: Little, Brown, 1915). Hawes, *Children in Urban Society,* 250–53.

9. Quoted in Hawes, 253. Emphasis in original.

10. William A. Healy, *Mental Conflicts and Misconduct* (Boston: Little, Brown, 1917), quoted in Hawes, 254–55.

11. Hamilton Cravens, "Child Saving in the Age of Professionalism, 1915–1930," in *American Childhood: A Research Guide and Historical Handbook,* ed. Joseph M. Hawes and N. Ray Hiner (Westport, Conn.: Greenwood Press, 1985), 417. See chapter 5 of this study for further discussion of the workings of the juvenile court and other social agencies that dealt with children. The Federal Children's Bureau, which was an advocate of courts, is discussed at length in chapter 4, and the rise of child science is treated in chapter 6.

12. David Nasaw, "Children and Commercial Culture: Motion Pictures in the Early Twentieth Century," in *Small Worlds: Children and Adolescents in America, 1850–1950,* ed. Elliot West and Paula Petrik (Lawrence: University Press of Kansas, 1992), 14–25. See also Nasaw, *Going Out: The Rise and Fall of Public Amusements* (New York: Basic Books, 1993) and Nasaw, *Children of the City.*

13. This discussion is based loosely on David Nasaw, *Children of the City,* and on John Clark, "The Stoop is the World," in *Growing Up in America,* ed. N. Ray Hiner and Joseph Hawes (Urbana: University of Illinois Press, 1985).

14. Viviana Zelizer, *Pricing the Priceless Child: The Changing Social Value of Children* (New York: Basic Books, 1985), 21.

15. Douglas A. Thom, "Habit Clinics for Children of the Pre-School Age," in Bremner et al., *Children and Youth in America: A Documentary History,* vol. 2, 1052.

16. Jane Addams, *The Spirit of Youth and the City Streets* (New York: Macmillan, 1930).

17. For a discussion of the impact of the depression on children and family life see chapter 7. See also Clark, "The Stoop Is the World," in Hiner and Hawes, *Growing Up in America.*

18. See Kathy Peiss, *Cheap Amusements: Working Women and Leisure in Turn-of-the-Century New York* (Philadelphia: Temple University Press, 1986) and Regina Kunzel, *Fallen Women, Problem Girls: Unmarried Mothers and the Professionalization of Social Work, 1890–1945* (New Haven and London: Yale University Press, 1993).

19. Elizabeth Ewen, *Immigrant Women in the Land of Dollars: Life and Culture on the Lower East Side, 1890–1925* (New York: Monthly Review Press, 1985), 216–24; Robert Sklar, *Movie-Made America, A Cultural History of American Movies* (New York: Random House, 1975), 130–40; Nasaw, *Going Out,* 227–40.

20. Quoted in Sklar, 138.

21. Nasaw, *Going Out,* 104–19, 241–42; Beth Bailey, *From Front Porch to Back Seat: Courtship in Twentieth-Century America* (Baltimore: Johns Hopkins University Press, 1988), 17–18.

22. Newspaper clipping, dated May 1922, in "History of the Michigan Congress of Parents and Teachers," by Mrs. William T. Sanders, January 1946. Box 10, Michigan Congress of Parents and Teachers. Records, Bentley Historical Library, University of Michigan.

23. Bailey, 22–26.

24. Mary Margaret Rutherford, "A Group of Fifty Senior Girls Who Are Enrolled at the University Neighborhood Centers, and a Group of Fifty Senior Girls Who Live in the Area of This Agency but Who Are Not Members. A Study of the Leisure Time Habits, Interests, and Group Affiliations of These Two Groups of Girls" (M.S. thesis, School of Applied Social Sciences, Western Reserve University, May 1938), 42; in University Settlement Papers, Western Reserve Historical Society, Cleveland, Ohio.

25. Ruth Alexander, " 'The Only Thing I Wanted Was Freedom': Wayward Girls in New York, 1900–1930," in West and Petrik, *Small Worlds,* 275–95. See also Joan Meyerowitz, "Sexual Geography and Gender Economy: The Furnished Room Districts of Chicago, 1890–1930," in *Gender and American History since 1890,* ed. Barbara Melosh (London and New York: Routledge, 1993) and Kathy Peiss, *Cheap Amusements.*

26. Constance Nathanson, *Dangerous Passage: The Social Control of Sexuality in Women's Adolescence* (Philadelphia: Temple University Press, 1991), 94–95.

27. Paula Fass, *The Damned and the Beautiful: American Youth in the 1920s* (New York: Oxford University Press, 1979), 6.

28. Bailey, 17.

29. John Modell, *Into One's Own: From Youth to Adulthood in the United States, 1920–1975* (Berkeley: University of California Press, 1989), 95.

30. See Christopher Lasch, *Haven in a Heartless World: The Family Besieged* (New York: Basic Books, 1977), 56–58.

31. Modell, 119.

32. quoted in Fass, 264.

33. Fass 266–67.

34. Fass, *Damned and Beautiful,* 270–76. The quotation is from 271.

35. Barbara Epstein, "Family Sexual Morality and Popular Movements in Turn-of-the-Century America," in *Powers of Desire: The Politics of Sexual-*

ity, ed. Ann Snitlow et al. (New York: Monthly Review Press, 1983) 117–30.

36. Modell, 135–53.
37. For a discussion of the construction of "whiteness," see Nasaw, *Going Out.*
38. Allison Davis and John Dollard, *Children of Bondage: The Personality Development of Negro Youth in the Urban South* (American Council on Education, ca. 1940; reprint, New York: Harper and Row, 1964), 266–68. See also E. Franklin Frazier, *Negro Youth at the Crossways: Their Personality Development in the Middle States* (Washington, D. C.: American Council on Education, 1940); Jay David, ed., *Growing Up Black: From Slave Days to the Present—25 African Americans Reveal the Trials and Triumphs of Their Childhoods* (New York: Avon Books, 1992); Patricia Riley, ed., *Growing Up Native American: An Anthology* (New York: William Morrow, 1993); Tiffany Lopez, ed., *Growing Up Chicano* (New York: William Morrow, 1993), and Selma Cantor Berrol, *Growing Up American: Immigrant Children in America Then and Now* (New York: Twayne Publishers, 1995).
39. For an autobiography describing what it was like to grow up in a poor African-American family in the deep South, see Anne Moody, *Coming of Age in Mississippi* (New York: Dell, 1968).
40. Glen H. Elder, *Children of the Great Depression: Social Change in Life Experience* (Chicago: University of Chicago Press, 1974), 75–85 .
41. Michael Church, "Michigan Youth During the Depression," Box 10, Michael Church Papers, Bentley Historical Library, University of Michigan.
42. William E. Leuchtenburg, *Franklin D. Roosevelt and the New Deal, 1932–1940* (New York: Harper and Row, 1963), 26–29.
43. Elder, 80.
44. quoted in Church, "Michigan Youth."
45. *Left Review* (published by the University of Michigan Branch of the Young Communist League), no. 3 (2 May 1939); copy in Michael Church Papers, Bentley Historical Library, box 10.
46. Sonya Alice Michel, "Children's Interests/Mother's Rights: Women, Professionals, and the American Family, 1920–1945" (Ph.D. diss., Brown University, 1986), 114.
47. Michel, 138–57.
48. Church, "Michigan Youth During the Depression."
49. Conference on Children and Youth in a Democracy, *Final Report* (Washington, D.C.: Government Printing Office, 1940).

Chapter 3

1. Paula S. Fass, *Outside In: Minorities and the Transformation of American Education* (New York: Oxford University Press, 1989), 20–25.

2. Social Science Research Council, *The Statistical History of the United States from Colonial Times to the Present* (Stamford, Conn.: Fairfield Publishers, 1965), 7, table H-223–H-233, "Elementary and Secondary School Enrollment and Attendance, and High School Graduates: 1870–1956," 207, table A 1–3, "Estimated Population of the United States: 1790–1957."

3. Christopher Jencks and David Riesman, *The Academic Revolution* (Garden City, N.Y.: Doubleday, 1968), 77, table 2, "Per Cent of All Individuals Born in Given Years Finishing High School and College: 1855–1944."

4. Ibid., 94–95.

5. Margaret Connell Szasz, "Federal Boarding Schools and the Indian Child, 1920–1960," in *Growing Up in America: Children in Historical Perspective,* ed. N. Ray Hiner and Joseph Hawes (Chicago and Urbana: University of Illinois Press, 1985), 209–18.

6. Basil Johnson, "A Day in the Life of Spanish," in *Growing Up Native American: An Anthology,* ed. Patricia Riley (New York: William Morrow, 1993), 172.

7. Szasz, 212–13.

8. Fass, *Minorities,* 22–26; Selma Berrol, "Immigrant Children at School, 1880–1940," in *Small Worlds: Children and Adolescents in America, 1850–1950,* ed. Elliott West and Paula Petrik (Lawrence: University Press of Kansas, 1992), 42–60.

9. Berrol, "Immigrant Children," 45–50; Berrol, *Growing Up American: Immigrant Children in America Then and Now* (New York: Twayne, 1995), 44.

10. Berroll, "Immigrant Children," 50; Elizabeth Ewen, *Immigrant Women in the Land of Dollars: Life and Culture on the Lower East Side, 1890–1925* (New York: Monthly Review Press, 1985) 175–76.

11. David Mint, "Patterns of Public School Segregation, 1900–1940: A Comparison Study of New York City, New Rochelle, and New Haven," in *Schools in Cities: Consensus and Conflict in American Educational History,* ed. Ronald K. Goodenow and Diane Ravitch (New York and London: Holmes and Meier, 1983), 67–110. See also Paul J. Ringel, "Industrial Education in Fitchburg, Massachusetts, 1908–1928," in Goodenow and Ravitch, *Schools in Cities,* 45–65.

12. Berrol, *Growing Up American,* 44–46; Fass, *Minorities,* 34.

13. Lawrence A. Cremin, *American Education: The Metropolitan Experience, 1876–1980* (New York: Harper and Row, 1988), 135–36.

14. Ibid., 145–47.

15. Fass, *Minorities,* 37.

16. Paul Davis Chapman, *Schools as Sorters: Lewis M. Terman, Applied Psychology, and the Intelligence Testing Movement, 1890–1930* (New York

and London: New York University Press, 1988), 83–89; Fass, *Minorities,* 37.

17. David Tyack and Elisabeth Hansot, *Managers of Virtue: Public School Leadership in America, 1820–1980* (New York: Basic Books, 1982), 107–11.
18. Ibid., 123–28.
19. Ibid., 131–33.
20. Ibid., 146, 157.
21. Robert S. Lynd and Helen M. Lynd, *Middletown: A Study in American Culture* (New York, Harcourt, Brace and World, 1929), 181–84.
22. Ibid., 188–89.
23. Ronald D. Cohen, *Children of the Mill: Schooling and Society in Gary, Indiana, 1906–1960* (Bloomington and Indianapolis: Indiana University Press, 1990), 78–79.
24. Ibid., 14, 26–28.
25. Ibid., 83
26. Ibid., 92–94.
27. Ibid., 93–99.
28. Ibid., 106.
29. Ibid., 195–96.
30. Robert S. Lynd and Helen M. Lynd, *Middletown in Transition: A Study in Cultural Conflicts* (New York: Harcourt Brace and Co., 1937), 205–6.
31. Reed Ueda, *Avenues to Adulthood: The Origins of the High School and Social Mobility in an American Suburb* (Cambridge: Cambridge University Press, 1987), 200; Paul J. Ringel, "Industrial Education in Fitchburg, Massachusetts, 1908–1928," in Goodenow and Ravitch, *Schools in Cities,* 45–65.
32. Ueda, 205–19.
33. Cohen, 130–47.
34. Robert S. and Helen M. Lynd, *Middletown in Transition,* 208–10. Quotation on page 210.
35. Ibid., 211–12.
36. Quoted in ibid., 220–21. Italics supplied by the Lynds.
37. Ibid., 223–24.
38. Paula Fass, *The Damned and the Beautiful: American Youth in the 1920s* (New York: Oxford University Press, 1977), 124–28.
39. Fass, 129–30; Lawrence A. Cremin, *American Education: The Metropolitan Experience, 1876–1980* (New York: Harper and Row, 1988), 565. Barbara Miller Solomon, *In the Company of Educated Women: A History of Women and Higher Education in America* (New Haven and London: Yale University Press, 1985), 144, table 7B, "Radcliffe Freshman Admissions."

40. Fass, *Damned and Beautiful,* 133.
41. Solomon, 63, table 2, "Women Enrolled in Institutions of Higher Education, 1870–1980," and 64, table 3, "College Women as a Percentage of Young Women in the United States, 1870–1980."
42. Solomon, 145, 147; Fass, 134.
43. Solomon, 148. See also Richard A. Reiman, *The New Deal and American Youth* (Athens and London: University of Georgia Press, 1992), chap. 3.

Chapter 4

1. Robyn Muncy, *Creating a Female Dominion in American Reform, 1890–1935* (New York: Oxford University Press, 1991), 35–43. See also Kristie Lindenmeyer, *"A Right to Childhood": The U.S. Children's Bureau and Child Welfare, 1912–1946* (Urbana: University of Illinois Press, forthcoming).
2. Molly Ladd-Taylor, *Raising a Baby the Government Way: Mother's Letters to the Children's Bureau, 1915–1932* (New Brunswick, N.J.: Rutgers University Press, 1986), 5. For the early history of the Children's Bureau see Nancy Potishman Weiss, "Save the Children: A History of the Children's Bureau, 1903–1918," (Ph.D. diss., University of California–Los Angeles, 1974); Louis J. Covotsos, "Child Welfare and Social Progress: A History of the United States Children's Bureau, 1912–1935" (Ph.D. diss., University of Chicago, 1976); Molly Ladd-Taylor, *Mother Work: Women, Child Welfare, and the State, 1890–1930* (Urbana and Chicago: University of Illinois Press, 1994), chap. 3; and Lindenmeyer, *"A Right to Childhood."*
3. Muncy, 45–51.
4. Muncy, 55, 58; Ladd-Taylor, *Raising a Baby,* 8.
5. Muncy, 62.
6. Ladd-Taylor, *Babies,* 10–11; Walter Trattner, *Crusade for the Children: A History of the National Child Labor Committee and Child Labor Reform in America* (Chicago: Quadrangle Books, 1970), 133–34; *Hammer v. Dagenhart,* 247 U. S., 251–81.
7. Muncy, 76–82; Ellen F. Fitzpatrick, "Academics and Activists: Women Social Scientists and the Impulse for Reform, 1892–1920" (Ph.D. diss., Brandeis, 1981), 175.
8. Ladd-Taylor, *Babies,* 19, 20.
9. Muncy, 93–102.
10. Ladd-Taylor, *Mothers,* 165–76; See also Lindenmeyer, chap. 4.
11. Ladd-Taylor, *Mothers,* chap. 6. For an example of the kind of opposition to Sheppard-Towner fostered by physicians see Ladd-Taylor, *Babies,* 193–95. For a discussion of the workings of Sheppard-Towner on the local level in a poor state, see Elissa Miller, "A History of Nursing Education in Arkansas," (Ph.D. diss., Memphis State University, 1989).

12. Ladd-Taylor, *Mothers,* 180–82; Muncy, 109–13.

13. Ladd-Taylor, *Mothers,* 184–90; Muncy 124–40.

14. For a discussion of efforts to regulate child labor, see Jeremy Felt, *Hostages of Fortune: Child Labor Reform in New York State* (Syracuse, N.Y.: Syracuse University Press, 1965) and Walter Trattner, *Crusade for the Children: A History of the National Child Labor Committee and Child Labor Reform in America* (Chicago: Quadrangle Books, 1970).

15. See Dorothy Ross, *The Origins of American Social Science* (New York: Cambridge University Press, 1991), especially chap. 10.

16. Nancy Pottishman Weiss, "Mother, the Invention of Necessity: Dr. Benjamin Spock's *Baby and Child Care,*" In *Growing Up in America,* ed. N. Ray Hiner and Joseph Hawes (Urbana: University of Illinois Press, 1985), 286; Ladd-Taylor, *Mothers,* 83–84.

17. Ladd-Taylor, *Mothers,* 83–84.

18. Quotations are from letters reprinted in Ladd-Taylor, *Baby,* 76–79.

19. Quoted in ibid., 86–91. See also Weiss, "Mother."

20. Quotations from Ladd-Taylor, *Baby,* 115–26.

21. Quoted in Ibid., 139–40; 150–51.

22. Leroy Ashby, *Saving the Waifs: Reformers and Dependent Children, 1890–1917* (Philadelphia: Temple University Press, 1984), 11; Ladd-Taylor, *Mothers,* chap. 5; U.S. Children's Bureau, *Standards of Public Aid to Children in Their Own Homes,* Publication No. 118 (Washington, D.C.: Government Printing Office, 1923).

23. Ladd-Taylor, *Mothers,* 160.

24. Dorothy E. Bradbury, *Five Decades of Action for Children: A History of the Children's Bureau* (Washington, D.C.: Social Security Administration, Children's Bureau, 1962; reprint, New York: Arno Press, 1974), 21–22; Lydia Roberts, *The Nutrition and Care of Children in a Mountain County of Kentucky* (U. S. Children's Bureau Publication No. 110, Washington, D.C.: Government Printing Office, 1922); U.S. Children's Bureau, *Maternal Deaths: Brief Report of a Study Made in Fifteen States* (Publication No. 221, Washington, D.C.: Government Printing Office, 1933)—both reprinted (New York: Arno Press, 1974). See also Lindenmeyer, chap. 6.

25. Bradbury, 26–27.

26. U.S. Children's Bureau, *Maternal Deaths,* 4–9, 59–60; Bradbury, 27–28.

27. Bradbury, 33–34. See also Dorothy Zeitz, *Child Welfare: Principles and Methods* (New York: John Wiley and Sons, 1959), 136; and Grace Abbott, "The County versus the Community as an Administrative Unit," *Social Service Review* (March 1930): 12–16.

28. Bradbury, 37–38; Zeitz, 136–37. See also Katherine F. Lenroot and Emma O. Lundberg, *Juvenile Courts at Work* (U. S Children's Bureau

Publication No. 141, Washington, D.C.: Government Printing Office, 1925).

29. Grace Abbott to Mrs. S. B., 22 May 1930, File 7-6-1-3, Children's Bureau Records, Central Files, 1929–1932, Records Group 102, Industrial and Social Branch, National Archives. Mrs. B's letter, File 8-2-1-4, is attached.

30. Abbott to Dr. A. J. Ostheimer, 12 January 1924, File 4-13-0, Children's Bureau Records, Central Files, 1921–1924, Records Group 102, Industrial and Social Branch, National Archives. The other letters are attached.

31. Anderson to Lundberg, 29 October 1924, File 4-13-2, Children's Bureau Records, Central Files, 1921–1924. Other letters are attached. See V. R. Anderson to Miss Mary Burge, R.N., 25 October 1927, File 7-6-0-1, Children's Bureau Records, Central Files, 1925–1928, for a typical response. The full citation for Gesell's work is Arnold Gesell, *The Retarded Child: How to Help Him* (Bloomington, Ill.: Public School Publishing Company, 1925).

32. Hanna to McCloy, 12 December 1929, File 7-6-0, Children's Bureau Records, Central Files, 1929–1932, McCloy letter attached.

33. Bradbury, 42–43; Ladd-Taylor, *Mothering,* 197–99. See also Lindenmeyer, chap. 7.

34. For a discussion of children's health issues in rural areas, see chap. 7.

35. Bradbury, 44–46.

36. Ibid., 47–48.

37. Ibid., 49–50.

38. Hann to Murphy, 12 May 1933, File 4-12-7-1-4, Children's Bureau Records, Central Files, 1933–1936. Murphy's letter is attached.

39. Oppenheimer to Bean, 20 May 1933, File 4-12-0, Children's Bureau Records, Central Files, 1933–1936. Bean's letters and scheme are attached.

40. Oppenheimer to Farler, 5 September 1935, File 4-12-7-2, Children's Bureau Records, Central Files, 1933–1936.

Chapter 5

1. For a discussion of this process, see Joseph Kett, *Rites of Passage: Adolescence in America, 1790 to the Present* (New York: Basic Books, 1977).

2. Hamilton Cravens, *Before Head Start: The Iowa Station and America's Children* (Chapel Hill and London: University of North Carolina Press, 1993), 68–69.

3. The literature on this last point is enormous and very compelling. See, for example, Rosalind Rosenberg, *Beyond Separate Spheres: The Intellectual Roots of Modern Feminism* (New Haven: Yale University Press,

1982); Margaret M. Caffrey, *Ruth Benedict: Stranger in This Land* (Austin: University of Texas Press, 1989); and Nancy Cott, *The Grounding of Modern Feminism* (New Haven: Yale University Press, 1987).

4. The preeminent scholar of the emergence of child science in the United States is Hamilton Cravens, whose major works on the subject include *Before Head Start* and "Child Saving in an Age of Professionalism," in *American Childhood: A Research Guide and Reference Handbook,* ed. Joseph M. Hawes and N. Ray Hiner (Westport, Conn.: Greenwood Press, 1985).

5. The best treatment of the child guidance movement in the 1920s and 1930s is Margo Horn, *Before It's Too Late: The Child Guidance Movement in the United States, 1922–1945* (Philadelphia: Temple University Press, 1989). The quotation is from p. 4.

6. Joseph M. Hawes, *Children in Urban Society: Juvenile Delinquency in the Nineteenth Century* (New York: Oxford University Press, 1971), 248–57; William A. Healy, *Mental Conflicts and Misconduct* (Boston: Little, Brown and Co., 1917), 2; William A. Healy, *The Practical Value of Scientific Study of Juvenile Delinquents,* Children's Bureau Publication No. 96 (Washington, D.C.: Government Printing Office, 1922); Horn, 11–15.

7. Horn, 23.

8. Robert R. Sears, *Your Ancients Revisited: A History of Child Development* (Chicago and London: University of Chicago Press, 1975), 16. See also Kathleen W. Jones, "Children and Child Guidance in the 1930s: The Juvenile 'Negotiators,' " unpublished MS, courtesy of the author.

9. In 1922, when the Commonwealth Fund demonstration clinics began, there were four psychiatric clinics treating children in operation in the United States: the Juvenile Psychopathic Institute of Chicago, founded in 1909; the outpatient department of the Boston Psychopathic Hospital, founded in 1912; the Henry Phipps Psychiatric Clinic at Johns Hopkins University, founded in 1913; and the Judge Baker Child Guidance Center in Boston, which opened in 1917 (Horn, 57).

10. Horn, 57–58.

11. Cleveland Children's Aid Society, Records, Western Reserve Historical Society, Cleveland, Ohio, box 1, folder 2.

12. Willard Olson, interview by Milton J. E. Senn, Senn Interviews in Child Development, National Library of Medicine (NLM), Bethesda, Maryland.

13. Horn, 39–40.

14. Horn, 85, 92–93.

15. 18 June 1939, Dr. Dorothy G. Sproul, M.D., to Dr. Harry Beal Torrey, Re: Guidance Clinic at East Bay Hospital, Jean MacFarlane Papers,

Archives of the History of Psychology, University of Akron, box 2106 (Hereafter cited as HPA).

16. Horn, 161.
17. Horn, 175–76; Jones, 4–5; Sonya Alice Michel, "Children's Interests/ Mother's Rights: Women, Professionals, and the American Family, 1920–1945" (Ph.D. diss., Brown University 1986), 57–114.
18. Summary of conference proceedings, 18 August 1938. U.S. Children's Bureau Central File, Records Group 102, National Archives; hereafter cited as CB.
19. For a discussion of the role of schools in the period, see chapter 3.
20. Christopher Lasch, *Haven in a Heartless World: The Family Besieged* (New York: Basic Books, 1977), 15.
21. Michel, 12–13.
22. Hamilton Cravens, "Child Saving in the Age of Professionalism, 1915–1930," in Hawes and Hiner, eds., *American Childhood,* 439, 446–47; For a much fuller treatment of Frank's role, see Cravens, *Before Head Start.*
23. "Lawrence K. Frank" interview by Milton J. Senn, Child Development Interviews, National Library of Medicine, Bethesda, Md. Hereafter cited as NLM interviews.
24. Cravens, "Child Saving," 439, 445; Cravens, *Before Head Start,* chaps. 1–5.
25. G. Stanley Hall, "The Contents of Children's Minds," *Princeton Review* (May 1883): 249–72; Hall, *Adolescence: Its Psychology, and Its Relations to Physiology, Anthropology, Sociology, Sex, Crime, Religion, and Education* (New York: D. Appleton, 1905); Dorothy G. Ross, *G. Stanley Hall: The Psychologist as Prophet* (Chicago: University of Chicago Press, 1972), 306; Edwin G. Boring, *A History of Experimental Psychology,* 2d ed. (New York: Appleton-Century-Crofts, 1950), 324.
26. James Mark Baldwin, *Mental Development in the Child and the Race: Methods and Processes* (New York: Macmillan, 1895) ix, 360.
27. Millicent Shinn, *The Biography of a Baby* (Boston: Houghton Mifflin, 1900), 10, 11; Gardiner Murphy, *Historical Introduction to Modern Psychology,* rev. ed. (New York: Harcourt Brace, 1949), 391.
28. George Dykhuizen, *The Life and Mind of John Dewey* (Carbondale, Ill.: Southern Illinois University Press, 1972), 55, 83–84; John Dewey, "The Reflex Arc Concept in Psychology," (1896) in John Dewey, *The Early Works 1882–1898* (Carbondale, Ill.: Southern Illinois University Press, 1972), v, 99–122; John Dewey, *School and Society* (Chicago: University of Chicago Press, 1900), 30, 31, 62, 63, 70; John Dewey, "The Psychological Aspect of the School Curriculum," *Educational Review* (April 1897): 364–66.
29. Edward L. Thorndike, *Educational Psychology* (New York: Lemche and Buechner, 1903), 3, 44–45, 94.

30. Cravens, *Before Head Start,* 42–53; Sears, *Your Ancients Revisited,* 42; John B. Watson, *Behavior: An Introduction to Comparative Psychology* (New York: Henry Holt, 1914); Watson, *Psychology from the Standpoint of a Behaviorist* (Philadelphia: J. B. Lippincott, 1919).

31. Nancy Pottisham Weiss, "Mother, the Invention of Necessity: Dr. Benjamin Spock's *Baby and Child Care,*" in *Growing Up in America: Children in Historical Perspective,* ed. N. Ray Hiner and Joseph M. Hawes (Urbana: University of Chicago Press, 1985), 290.

32. Cravens, *Before Head Start,* 83, 93–99. The quotation is on p. 98.

33. Cravens, *Before Head Start,* 99–100; Nancy Bayley, interview with Milton J. E. Senn, 30 October 1969, Child Development Interviews, NLM. There were three long-term longitudinal studies at the Institute of Child Welfare at the University of California–Berkeley. The Guidance Study, under Jean W. Macfarlane, sought to test the usefulness of "intensive and extensive discussion with parents about child-training procedures, family member personality characteristics, interpersonal relationships, health, background, social status, and so forth." The second, the Berkeley Growth Study, under Nancy Bayley and Lotta V. Wolff, was "designed as an intensive investigation of physical, mental, physiological, and motor development in the first 15 months of postpartum life." The third study, begun as the Adolescent Growth Study and renamed the Oakland Growth Study, under Harold E. Jones and Herbert R. Stolz, was designed to "investigate adolescent growth and change in a wide number of aspects." From Mary Cover Jones et al., eds., *The Course of Human Development: Selected Papers from the Longitudinal Studies, Institute of Human Development, The University of California, Berkeley* (Waltham, Mass.: Xerox College Publishing, 1971), 3–4.

34. Wayne Dennis, interview by Milton J. E. Senn, Child Development Interviews, NLM, 13 April 1971.

35. J. McVickar Hunt, interview by Milton J. E. Senn, Child Development Interviews, NLM, 9 June 1974, 2d interview.

36. Macfarlane to Gelolo McHugh, 17 November 1939, box 2106, Macfarlane Papers, HPA.

37. Attachment to Mary Ruth Colby to Florence Goodenough, 28 November 1939, CB.

38. Jones et al., eds., 104; Bayley, quoted in Jones et al., 105.

39. Sears, *Your Ancients Revisited,* 38–40; See the interview of Dennis in Interviews in Child Development, by Milton J. E. Senn, NLM.

40. quoted in Michel, 135–36.

41. Emma Johnson to Jean W. Macfarlane, 5 October 1939, Jean W. Macfarlane papers, HPA, Box 2106.

42. Macfarlane to Johnson, 10 October 1939, ibid.

43. Johnson to Macfarlane, 13 October 1939, ibid.

44. Address "The Pre-school Child from the Standpoint of Public Hygiene and Education" given at Mid West Conference on Parent Education, Chicago Association for Child Study and Parent Education, 6 March 1926. Gesell Papers, Box 141, Library of Congress. Hereafter cited as GP.
45. Ibid.
46. Catherine Landreth, letter to parents, 27 September 1929, Macfarlane papers, Box 2106, HPA.
47. Marjorie Merl Cluff, "An Inquiry into the Parent Education Programs of Nursery Schools in the United States" (M.S. thesis, Western Reserve University, 1932), 45.
48. Quoted in Michel, "Children's Interests/Mother's Rights," 184–85.
49. Michel, 186.
50. Angelo Patri, Papers, Manuscript Division, Library of Congress, Box 38; hereafter cited as AP.
51. Ibid., AP.
52. George Hecht, interview, Child Development Interviews, NLM.
53. This discussion based on Julia Grant, "Mothers Take on the Experts: The Cornell Child Study Clubs, 1925–45," unpublished paper; quotations are from the paper.
54. Myrtle McCraw, interview, 9 May 1972. Child Development Interviews, NLM.
55. GP, Box 159. Emphasis in original.
56. Willard Beatty to Lawrence K. Frank, 31 January 1938, Frank Papers, National Library of Medicine. Hereafter cited as FP.
57. Beatty to Frank, 2 December 1938, FP.
58. Macfarlane to Lawrence K. Frank on his 75th birthday, 9 March 1964, Box 2087, Macfarlane Papers, HPA.

Chapter 6

1. The work of the Children's Bureau is described in chapter 4, and the rise and development of child science is found in chapter 5. The impact of the depression and the New Deal is found in chapter 7, and the schools are treated in chapter 3.
2. Beverly Stadum, *Poor Women and Their Families: Hard Working Charity Cases, 1900–1930* (Albany: State University of New York Press, 1992), xxi–xxii.
3. Sonya Alice Michel, "Children's Interests/Mother's Rights: Women, Professionals, and the American Family, 1920–1945" (Ph.D. diss., Brown University, 1986), University Microfilms 8617598, 4–13.
4. Family Service Association of Cleveland Records, 1919–1971, Western Reserve Historical Society Serial #3920 Box 6, f 9—Minutes of the Home Economics Committee, entries for 20 February and 5 March 1920.

5. Ibid., minutes of 19 March, 2 April, 23 April, 11 June, 27 September, and 22 October 1920; 12 May 1922. The quotation is from 27 September 1920.
6. Ibid., minutes of 7 January and 4 February 1921. Quotation is from 18 March 1921.
7. Ibid., minutes of 1 April, 15 April, 29 April, and 3 June 1921.
8. Ibid., minutes of 15 April 1921, 4 November 1921, 20 January 1922, 20 April 1923, 19 October 1923.
9. Ibid., 8 February 1924.
10. Ibid., 21 March 1924, 4 April 1925.
11. Ibid., 2 May 1924.
12. Youth Service Records. Box 1 F 2 History, Western Reserve Historical Society, Cleveland, Ohio.
13. Ibid., Annual Report of the Medical Director, 1921.
14. Ibid., 1923 Annual Report.
15. Ibid., Annual Report, 1925.
16. Ibid., Annual Report of the Advisory Department, 1927,
17. Letter from Junior League, 21 October 1919, Cleveland Fund papers, Western Reserve Historical Society.
18. Linda Gordon, *Heroes of Their Own Lives: The Politics and History of Family Violence, Boston 1880–1960* (New York: Viking, 1988), 221.
19. Cleveland Children's Aid Society, Records, Historical Summary, Box 1, Western Reserve Historical Society.
20. Ibid., interview with Lawrence Cole, 1937, historical folder.
21. 1922–1923 Annual Report, 1925 Annual Report, YMCA of Metropolitan Detroit Papers, Bentley Library, University of Michigan, Box 1, Folder Annual Reports, 1920–1929.
22. Detroit YMCA 1925 Annual Report.
23. "Camps" in Ibid.
24. St. Antoine Branch Detroit YMCA Annual Report for 1929, ibid.
25. Ibid.
26. Cheryl Greenberg, *Or Does It Explode? Black Harlem in the Great Depression* (New York: Oxford University Press, 1991), 36–59.
27. Greenberg, 170–71; Andrew Billingsley and Jeanne Giovannoni, *Children of the Storm: Black Children and American Child Welfare* (New York: Harcourt, Brace and Jovanovich, 1972), 106–9.
28. Greenberg, 172–79; Billingsley, 106–7.
29. Margo Horn, "Inventing the Problem Child: 'At Risk' Children in the Child Guidance Movement of the 1920s and 1930s," in *Children at Risk in America: History, Concepts, and Public Policy,* ed. Roberta Wollons (Albany: State University of New York Press, 1993), 141–53; Margo Horn, *Before It's Too Late, The Child Guidance Movement in the United States, 1922–1945* (Philadelphia: Temple University Press, 1989) x, 4–9,

148 Children between the Wars: American Childhood, 1920–1940

34; Murray Levine and Adeline Levine, *Helping Children: A Social History* (New York: Oxford University Press, 1992), 144–61; George S. Stevenson, "Child Guidance and the National Committee for Mental Hygiene," in *Orthopsychiatry 1923–1948: Retrospect and Prospect,* ed. Lawson G. Lowery and Victoria Sloan (New York: American Orthopsychiatric Association, 1948) 50–82. See also chapter 5.

30. Joan Gittens, *Poor Relations: The Children of the State in Illinois, 1818–1990* (Urbana and Chicago: University of Illinois Press, 1994) 125–26.
31. ibid., 129–30.
32. Robert S. McElvaine, *The Great Depression: America, 1929–1941* (New York: Times Books, 1993 [c. 1984]), 75. For a discussion of the impact of the depression on children, see chapter 7.
33. Detroit YMCA Records, 1932 Annual Report.
34. Annual Reports for 1933, 1934, ibid.
35. Annual Reports for 1937, 1939, and 1940, ibid.
36. C. C. Carsten to William J. Norton, 30 January 1936, Norton Correspondence, Box 10, Children's Fund Papers, Bentley Historical Library, University of Michigan.
37. 30 September 1930, memorandum, Box 1, Dunham, Arthur, papers, Bentley Library, University of Michigan.
38. Home Economics Committee Minutes, 30 April 1931, Family Service Association Papers, Western Reserve Historical Society, Cleveland, Ohio.
39. Folder entitled "Save the Children Federation," Box 98, Papers of Henry J. Allen, Manuscript Division, Library of Congress.

Chapter 7

1. Robert S. McElvaine, *The Great Depression: America, 1929–1941* (New York: Times Books, 1993 [c. 1984]), 75.
2. Studs Terkel, *Hard Times: An Oral History of the Great Depression* (New York: Washington Square Press, 1970), 116–17.
3. Ibid., 120–22.
4. Leroy Ashby, "The Depression and World War II," in *American Childhood, A Research Guide and Historical Handbook,* ed. Joseph M. Hawes and N. Ray Hiner (Westport, Conn.: Greenwood Press, 1985), 506–7. Robert S. Lynd and Helen Merril Lynd, *Middletown in Transition: A Study in Cultural Conflicts* (New York: Harcourt Brace, 1937).
5. William E. Leuchtenburg, *Franklin Roosevelt and the New Deal, 1932–40* (New York: Harper and Row, 1963), 1.
6. See chapter 4.
7. Leuchtenburg, 111, 117. See Glen Elder, *Children of the Great Depression: Social Change in Life Experience* (Chicago: University of Chicago Press, 1974), 64.

8. Elder, 80.
9. Leuchtenburg, 26–29.
10. Colin Gordon, *New Deals: Business, Labor, and Politics in America, 1920–1935* (New York: Cambridge University Press, 1994), 161–67; See also Irving Bernstein, *A Caring Society: The New Deal, the Worker, and the Great Depression* (Boston: Houghton Mifflin, 1985).
11. Family Service Association of Cleveland, Records, 1919–1971. Western Reserve Historical Society Collection #3920 Box 6, f 9—Minutes of the Home Economics Committee.
12. Youth Service records, WRHS #3629 Box 1. See, for example, the case discussed on 18 April 1935 regarding a girl who was judged to be in danger of becoming a prostitute.
13. Youth Service, Box 3, scrapbooks, WRHS Cleveland Press, 18 January 1933.
14. Box 10, Children's Fund of Michigan Papers, Bentley Historical Library, University of Michigan, Ann Arbor, Michigan.
15. Winnifred Golley to William J. Norton, 22 July 1940, Box 10, Children's Fund of Michigan Papers, Bentley Historical Library, University of Michigan, Ann Arbor, Michigan.
16. Red Johnson to William J. Norton, Box 15, Children's Fund Papers, Bentley Library.
17. "Annual Report of the Research Laboratory, Children's Fund of Michigan, 1934–35," 19, Icie Macy Hoobler papers, Bentley Historical Library, Box 6.
18. On Couzens see Robert E. Conot, *American Odyssey* (New York: William Morrow, 1974), xxii, 275–76, 305; speech, "The Children's Fund of Michigan," 10 January 1933, William J. Norton Papers, Bentley Library, Box 1.
19. Sally D. Benjamin, "The Merrill Palmer Institute: Its Formative Role in the Beginnings of the Scientific Study of the Child Development" (Senior honors thesis, University of Michigan, 1980), 88, 90.
20. Willis Frederick Dunbar, *Michigan: A History of the Wolverine State* (Grand Rapids, Mich.: Willis B. Eerdemans Publishing, 1970), 679. See the Norton Papers or the Children's Fund Papers for many examples of requests to which the Children's Fund responded.
21. Norton, speech of 10 January 1933; Dunbar, 706. During the 1930s, many counties in Michigan maintained their own teacher training or "normal" schools, providing potential teachers with a year's training after eighth grade graduation. See Dunbar, *A History of the Wolverine State*, 706.
22. Children's Fund of Michigan, Eighth Annual Report, 1936–1937; Eleventh Annual Report, 1939–1940, 10, Box 1, Children's Fund Papers, Bentley Library.

23. "Report of the Nursing Service, July, 1930," Box 4, Children's Fund Papers, Bentley Library.

24. Ibid.

25. Golley to Norton, 22 July 1940, Box 10, Children's Fund Papers, Bentley Library, attachment.

26. Annual Report, Child Health Division 1931–1932, and Annual Report, Child Health Division, 1932–1933, Box 4, Children's Fund Papers, Bentley Library.

27. J. Stanley Lemons, "The Sheppard-Towner Act: Progressivism in the 1920s," *Journal of American History* 65 (1969): 776–86. See also Charles King, *Children's Health in America: A History* (New York: Twayne, 1993), 138–39.

28. Social Science Research Council, *The Statistical History of the United States from Colonial Times to the Present* (Stamford, Conn.: Fairfield Publishers, 1965), 25, table B 101–112, "Fetal Death Ratios: Neonatal, Infant, and Maternal Mortality Rates, by Color: 1915–1956."

29. I am indebted to Professor Leo Graff of Aquinas College for pointing out the importance of this figure.

30. Child Health Division Summary, 1940–1941, Box 4, Children's Fund Papers, Bentley Library; Dunbar, 636.

31. Annual Report of the Research Laboratory, Children's Fund of Michigan, 1934–1935, Box 6, Report of the Annual Meeting of the Society for Research in Child Development, 1934, Box 21, Hoobler papers, Bentley Library.

32. Macy to Dr. Lafayette Mendel, Professor of Physiological Chemistry at Yale (her mentor), 7 March 1934; Mendel to Macy, 16 May 1934, Box 25, Hoobler Papers, Bentley Library.

33. Colby to Macy, 4 May 1936, Box 8, Hoobler Papers. See also Colby, Walter Francis Papers, Box 1, Bentley Library, University of Michigan. Colby was a physicist at Michigan, and his wife a psychologist. Box 1 includes a list of Martha Guernsey Colby's publications.

34. Macy to Auerbacher, 18 December 1934, Box 6, Hoobler papers, Bentley Library.

35. Report of the Annual Meeting, Society for Research in Child Development, December 1934, Box 21, Hoobler papers, Bentley Library. On Daniels's research, see Cravens, 84–85.

36. I am indebted to Professor Marsha Walton of the Psychology Department at Rhodes College for this point. See also Jan Riordan and Kathleen G. Auerbach, *Breastfeeding and Human Lactation* (Boston and London: Jones and Bartlett Publishers, 1993), 114.

37. Leuchtenburg, 46–54, 120–24.

38. Joseph M. Hawes, *The Children's Rights Movement: A History of Advocacy and Protection* (Boston: Twayne, 1991), 69–73. The standard

treatment of the NYA is Richard Reiman, *The New Deal and American Youth: Ideas and Ideals in a Depression Decade* (Athens: University of Georgia Press, 1992).

39. Leuchtenburg, 97–98.
40. Mary McLeod Bethune to Aubrey Williams, 10 June 1938, NYA Records, quoted in Bremner et al., *Children and Youth in America,* vol. 3 (Cambridge, Mass.: Harvard University Press, 1974), 87.
41. Paul B. Jacobson, "End of N. Y. A.," *School Review* 51 (1943): 454–56; quoted in Bremner et al., vol. 3, 90–91.
42. Hawes, *Children's Rights,* 71–72.
43. U.S. Children's Bureau, "Security for Children," staff study included in U.S. Committee on Economic Security, *Social Security in America: The Factual Background of Social Security Act as Summarized from the Staff Reports to the Committee on Economic Security,* Social Security Board Publication No. 20 (Washington, D.C.: 1937); quoted in Bremner et al., vol. 3, 525–27.
44. Leuchtenburg, 132–33. See also Walter Trattner, *From Poor Law to Welfare State: A History of Social Welfare in America* (New York: Free Press, 1974), 242.
45. Ashby in Hawes and Hiner, 496. For an extended discussion of this problem see "Rights of Children under AFDC," in Bremner et al., vol. 3, 576–619.
46. Ashby in Hawes and Hiner, 499–500.
47. Bremner et al., vol. 3, 722–27. The standard history of day care is Margaret O'Brien Steinfels, *Who's Minding the Children? The History and Politics of Day Care in America* (New York: Simon and Schuster), 1973.
48. Edna Ewing Kelley, "Uncle Sam's Nursery Schools," *Parents Magazine* (March, 1936), quoted in Bremner et al., vol. 3, 680–81.
49. U.S. Federal Works Agency, *Final Report on the WPA Program, 1935–1943* (Washington, D.C.: 1947) quoted in Bremner et al., vol. 3, 681.

Bibliographic Essay

General Works (Chapter 1)

There are several guides to the literature regarding children and childhood in the United States, including Joseph M. Hawes and N. Ray Hiner, *American Childhood: A Research Guide and Historical Handbook* (Westport, Conn., and London: Greenwood Press, 1985); N. Ray Hiner and Joseph Hawes, *Growing Up in America* (Urbana: University of Illinois Press, 1985); and Robert Bremner et al., eds., *Children and Youth in America: A Documentary History* (Cambridge, Mass: Harvard University Press, 1970–1974). This last work is much more than a guide to the literature, as it is also a comprehensive documentary history of American childhood. For a broader worldwide historical view of childhood, see Joseph M. Hawes and N. Ray Hiner, *Children in Historical and Comparative Perspective* (Westport, Conn., and London: Greenwood Press, 1991). The chapter about the United States updates *American Childhood*. See also Elliott West and Paula Petrik, eds., *Small Worlds: Children and Adolescents in America, 1850–1950* (Lawrence: University Press of Kansas, 1992) and two works by Harvey J. Graff, *Conflicting Paths: Growing Up in America* (Cambridge, Mass., and London: Harvard University Press, 1995) and *Growing Up in America: Historical Experiences* (Detroit: Wayne State University Press, 1987). The former work by Graff, being monographic in nature, has an extensive citations to recent literature.

There are other works that, although somewhat broader in scope, treat the interwar period in some depth, such as Joseph M. Hawes, *The Children's Rights Movement: A History of Advocacy and Protection* (Boston: Twayne, 1991); Viviana Zelizer, *Pricing the Priceless Child: The Changing Social Value of Children* (New York: Basic Books, 1985); Steven Mintz and Susan Kellogg, *Domestic Revolutions: A Social History of American Family Life* (New York: Free Press, 1988); W. Norton Grubb and Marvin Lazerson, *Broken Promises: How Americans Fail Their Children* (New York: Basic Books, 1982); Elizabeth

Ewen, *Immigrant Women in the Land of Dollars: Life and Culture on the Lower East Side, 1890–1925* (New York: Monthly Review Press, 1985); and John Modell, *Into One's Own: From Youth to Adulthood in the United States, 1920–1975* (Berkeley: University of California Press, 1989).

Some of the best treatments of children in the period remain in unpublished form. Notable in this literature are Sonya Michel, "Children's Interests/Mother's Rights: Women, Professionals, and the American Family, 1920–1945" (Ph.D. diss., Brown University, 1986) and Ellen F. Fitzpatrick, "Academics and Activists: Women Social Scientists and the Impulse for Reform, 1892–1920" (Ph.D. diss., Brandeis, 1981). A variety of other works touch on the period, including Margo Horn, *Before It's Too Late: The Child Guidance Movement in the United States, 1922–1945* (Philadelphia: Temple University Press, 1989); Sheila Rothman, *Woman's Proper Place: A History of Changing Ideology and Practice, 1870 to the Present* (New York: Basic Books, 1978); Joseph Kett, *Rites of Passage: Adolescence in America, 1790 to the Present* (New York: Basic Books, 1977); Nancy Cott, *The Grounding of Modern Feminism* (New Haven: Yale University Press, 1987); and Molly Ladd-Taylor, *Women, Child Welfare, and the State* (Urbana: University of Illinois Press, 1994). For an overview of the period as a whole, see Sean Dennis Cashman, *America in the Twenties and Thirties: The Olympian Age of Franklin Delano Roosevelt* (New York and London: New York University Press, 1989).

Children's Culture (Chapter 2)

A work of profound significance that discusses children's culture extensively is David Nasaw, *Children of the City at Work and at Play* (Garden City, N.Y.: Anchor/Doubleday, 1985). Other works by Nasaw, "Children and Commercial Culture: Motion Pictures in the Early Twentieth Century," in *Small Worlds: Children and Adolescents in America, 1850–1950*, ed. Elliott West and Paula Petrik (Lawrence: University Press of Kansas, 1992), 14–25; and *Going Out: The Rise and Fall of Public Amusements* (New York: Basic Books, 1993) are equally impressive and important. No other scholar has done as much to explain the interaction between children and American society in the early twentieth century. A work that supplements Nasaw and confirms his insights is John Clark, "The Stoop Is the World," in *Growing Up in America*, ed. N. Ray Hiner and Joseph Hawes (Urbana: University of Illinois Press, 1985).

Works that deal with the realities of city life and how young people dealt with them include Kathy Peiss, *Cheap Amusements: Working Women and Leisure in Turn-of-the-Century New York* (Philadelphia: Temple University Press, 1986); Regina Kunzel, *Fallen Women, Problem Girls: Unmarried Mothers and the Professionalization of Social Work, 1890–1945* (New Haven and London: Yale University Press, 1993); Eric C. Schneider, *In the Web of Class: Delinquents and Reformers in Boston, 1810–1930s* (New York and London:

New York University Press, 1992); Ruth Alexander, " 'The Only Thing I Wanted Was Freedom': Wayward Girls in New York, 1900–1930," in West and Petrik, *Small Worlds,* 275–95; Joan Meyerowitz, "Sexual Geography and Gender Economy: The Furnished Room Districts of Chicago, 1890–1930," in *Gender and American History since 1890,* by Barbara Melosh (London and New York: Routledge, 1993); Constance Nathanson, *Dangerous Passage: The Social Control of Sexuality in Women's Adolescence* (Philadelphia: Temple University Press, 1991); Elizabeth Ewen, *Immigrant Women in the Land of Dollars: Life and Culture on the Lower East Side, 1890–1925* (New York: Monthly Review Press, 1985); Mary E. Odem, *Delinquent Daughters: Protecting and Policing Adolescent Female Sexuality in the United States, 1885–1920* (Chapel Hill and London: University of North Carolina Press, 1995).

Juvenile Courts and their workings have been thoroughly studied. Among the works treating the origins and spread of the courts are Joseph M. Hawes, *Children in Urban Society: Juvenile Delinquency in the Nineteenth Century* (New York: Oxford University Press, 1971); Justine Wise Polier, *Everyone's Children, Nobody's Child: A Judge Looks at Underprivileged Children in the United States* (New York: Charles Scribner's Sons, 1941); Ellen Ryerson, *The Best Laid Plans: America's Juvenile Court Experiment* (New York: Hill and Wang, 1978); Stephen Schlossman, *Love and the American Delinquent: The Theory and Practice of "Progressive" Juvenile Justice, 1825–1920* (Chicago: University of Chicago Press, 1977); and John R. Sutton, *Stubborn Children: Controlling Delinquency in the United States, 1640–1981* (Berkeley: University of California Press, 1988). A specialized treatment that looks at the relationship between the courts and the development of child science is Hamilton Cravens, "Child Saving in the Age of Professionalism, 1915–1930," in *American Childhood: A Research Guide and Historical Handbook,* ed. Joseph M. Hawes and N. Ray Hiner (Westport, Conn.: Greenwood Press, 1985).

There are a number of treatments of the rise of movies and radio in the period, including Robert Sklar, *Movie-Made America: A Cultural History of American Movies* (New York: Random House, 1975); and J. Fred MacDonald, *Don't Touch That Dial! Radio Programming in American Life from 1920 to 1960* (Chicago: Nelson-Hall, 1980).

Several works discuss the rise of youth peer groups and the development of the social practice of dating. Among them are Beth Bailey, *From Front Porch to Back Seat: Courtship in Twentieth-Century America* (Baltimore: Johns Hopkins University Press, 1988); Paula Fass, *The Damned and the Beautiful: American Youth in the 1920s* (New York: Oxford University Press, 1979); John Modell, *Into One's Own: From Youth to Adulthood in the United States, 1920–1975* (Berkeley: University of California Press, 1989); and Barbara Epstein, "Family Sexual Morality and Popular Movements in

Turn-of-the-Century America," in *Powers of Desire: The Politics of Sexuality,* ed. Ann Snitlow, Christine Stansell, and Sharon Thompson (New York: Monthly Review Press, 1983).

The culture of immigrant and ethnic children has attracted the attention of scholars both during the period and since. The better works include Allison Davis and John Dollard, *Children of Bondage: The Personality Development of Negro Youth in the Urban South* (American Council on Education, ca. 1940; reprint, New York: Harper and Row, 1964); E. Franklin Frazier, *Negro Youth at the Crossways: Their Personality Development in the Middle States* (Washington, D. C.: American Council on Education, 1940); Jay David, ed., *Growing Up Black: From Slave Days to the Present—25 African Americans Reveal the Trials and Triumphs of Their Childhoods* (New York: Avon Books, 1992); Patricia Riley, ed., *Growing Up Native American: An Anthology* (New York: William Morrow, 1993); Tiffany Lopez, ed., *Growing Up Chicano* (New York: William Morrow, 1993); and Selma Cantor Berrol, *Growing Up American: Immigrant Children in America Then and Now* (New York: Twayne Publishers, 1995).

In a class by itself and easily one of the dominant works dealing with children and the depression is Glen H. Elder, *Children of the Great Depression: Social Change in Life Experience* (Chicago: University of Chicago Press, 1974). In addition to Elder's work, which is indispensable, see also the final report of the 1940 White House Conference on Children and Youth: Conference on Children and Youth in a Democracy, *Final Report* (Washington, D.C.: Government Printing Office, 1940).

Schools between the Wars (Chapter 3)

The magisterial concluding volume of Lawrence A. Cremin's multivolume history of American education, *American Education: The Metropolitan Experience, 1876–1980* (New York: Harper and Row, 1988) belongs at the top of any list of books pertaining to the interwar period. Also important for the period are Christopher Jencks and David Riesman, *The Academic Revolution* (Garden City, N.Y.: Doubleday, 1968); Ronald K. Goodenow and Diane Ravitch, eds., *Schools in Cities: Consensus and Conflict in American Educational History* (New York and London: Holmes and Meier, 1983); David Tyack and Elisabeth Hansot, *Managers of Virtue: Public School Leadership in America, 1820–1980* (New York: Basic Books, 1982); and David Tyack, *The One Best System: A History of American Urban Education* (Cambridge, Mass.: Harvard University Press, 1974).

The impact of schools on immigrants and minorities is part of the focus of Selma Berrol's "Immigrant Children at School, 1880–1940," in *Small Worlds: Children and Adolescents in America, 1850–1950,* ed. Elliott West and Paula Petrik (Lawrence: University Press of Kansas, 1992), 42–60; and her more comprehensive *Growing Up American: Immigrant Children in*

American Then and Now (New York: Twayne, 1995). Just as the schools had an impact on minorities, so they in turn affected the schools they attended, as Paula S. Fass explains in *Outside In: Minorities and the Transformation of American Education* (New York: Oxford University Press, 1989). Similarly, schools for Native Americans can be seen in terms of broad policy, as treated by Margaret Connell Szasz in "Federal Boarding Schools and the Indian Child, 1920–1960," in *Growing Up in America: Children in Historical Perspective*, ed. N. Ray Hiner and Joseph Hawes (Chicago and Urbana: University of Illinois Press, 1985), or from the perspective of the Native American children in attendance as in Basil Johnson's "A Day in the Life of Spanish," in *Growing Up Native American: An Anthology*, ed. Patricia Riley (New York: William Morrow, 1993).

The role of the schools and their broad social function is the subject of Paul Davis Chapman, *Schools as Sorters: Lewis M. Terman, Applied Psychology, and the Intelligence Testing Movement, 1890–1930* (New York and London: New York University Press, 1988), and the relationship between schools and the community receives considerable attention in Robert S. Lynd and Helen M. Lynd, *Middletown: A Study in American Culture* (New York: Harcourt, Brace and World, 1929), and the sequel, *Middletown in Transition: A Study in Cultural Conflicts* (New York: Harcourt Brace and Co., 1937). Combining aspects of the two in an important and persuasive work is Ronald D. Cohen's *Children of the Mill: Schooling and Society in Gary, Indiana, 1906–1960* (Bloomington and Indianapolis: Indiana University Press, 1990).

One of the major changes in American education in the period was the expansion of the high school and the creation of the junior high school. Best on the junior high school is Reed Ueda, *Avenues to Adulthood: The Origins of the High School and Social Mobility in an American Suburb* (Cambridge: Cambridge University Press, 1987), and the standard work on high schools is Edward A. Krug, *The Shaping of the American High School, 1920–1941* (Madison: University of Wisconsin Press, 1972). In *The Making of an American High School: The Credential Market and the Central High School of Philadelphia* (New Haven: Yale University Press, 1988), David F. Labaree looks at the changes in a single urban institution. To determine how classrooms changed or did not, Larry Cuban studied the pervasiveness of educational innovations in *How Teachers Taught: Constancy and Change in American Classrooms, 1890—1980* (New York: Longman, 1984).

Higher education expanded in the period, too, with the increased enrollment of women being one of the primary characteristics. The process is best analyzed in Barbara Miller Solomon's *In the Company of Educated Women: A History of Women and Higher Education in America* (New Haven and London: Yale University Press, 1985), and the changing mores of college youth are superbly treated by Paula Fass in *The Damned and the Beautiful: American Youth in the 1920s* (New York: Oxford University Press, 1977).

The Federal Children's Bureau (Chapter 4)

There have been several studies of the Federal Children's Bureau. The best and most recent is Kristie Lindenmeyer, *"A Right to Childhood": The U.S. Children's Bureau and Child Welfare, 1912–1946* (Urbana: University of Illinois Press, 1997). Two important dissertations have also looked at the bureau: Nancy Pottishman Weiss, "Save the Children: A History of the Children's Bureau, 1903–1918," (Ph.D. diss., University of California–Los Angeles, 1974), and Louis J. Covotsos, "Child Welfare and Social Progress: A History of the United States Children's Bureau, 1912–1935" (Ph.D. diss., University of Chicago, 1976). An older institutional history of the bureau is Dorothy E. Bradbury, *Five Decades of Action for Children: A History of the Children's Bureau* (Washington, D.C.: Social Security Administration, Children's Bureau, 1962). Another recent work, Molly Ladd-Taylor's *Raising a Baby the Government Way: Mother's Letters to the Children's Bureau, 1915–1932* (New Brunswick, N.J.: Rutgers University Press, 1986), is based on letters sent to and received by the Children's Bureau. The Children's Bureau Records are particularly rich and interesting; they are Records Group 102, Industrial and Social Branch in the National Archives.

A number of excellent histories of social welfare place the work of the bureau in context but treat its efforts at improving infant mortality rates through prenatal care (Sheppard-Towner) and the effort to regulate child labor. Among them, Robyn Muncy, *Creating a Female Dominion in American Reform, 1890–1935* (New York: Oxford University Press, 1991); Molly Ladd-Taylor, *Mother Work: Women, Child Welfare, and the State, 1890–1930* (Urbana and Chicago: University of Illinois Press, 1994); Linda Gordon, *Pitied but Not Entitled: Single Mothers and the History of Welfare, 1890–1935* (New York: Free Press, 1994) stand out, but see also the fine dissertations by Sonya Michel, "Children's Interests/Mother's Rights: Women, Professionals, and the American Family, 1920–1945" (Ph.D. diss., Brown University 1986); and Ellen F. Fitzpatrick, "Academics and Activists: Women Social Scientists and the Impulse for Reform, 1892–1920," (Ph.D. diss., Brandeis, 1981). The two classic works on the effort to regulate child labor are Walter Trattner, *Crusade for the Children: A History of the National Child Labor Committee and Child Labor Reform in America* (Chicago: Quadrangle Books, 1970), and Jeremy Felt, *Hostages of Fortune: Child Labor Reform in New York State* (Syracuse, N.Y.: Syracuse University Press, 1965). An interesting discussion of the child-rearing advice given by the bureau and the links between the bureau and Dr. Spock, the preeminent child-rearing expert of postwar America, is provided by Nancy Pottishman Weiss, "Mother, the Invention of Necessity: Dr. Benjamin Spock's *Baby and Child Care*," in *Growing Up in America,* ed. N. Ray Hiner and Joseph Hawes (Urbana: University of Illinois Press), 1985. Works touching on the period and on some of the bureau's work include Leroy Ashby, *Saving the Waifs: Reformers and Dependent Children, 1890–1917* (Philadelphia: Temple University Press, 1984) and Emma O. Lundberg, *Unto the Least of These: Social Services for Children* (New York: Appleton Century Crofts, 1947).

Child Science (Chapter 5)

The preeminent work describing the rise of child science in the United States in the 1920s and 1930s is Hamilton Cravens's *Before Head Start: The Iowa Station and America's Children* (Chapel Hill and London: University of North Carolina Press, 1993). See also his "Child Saving in the Age of Professionalism, 1915–1930," in *American Childhood: A Research Guide and Historical Handbook,* ed. Joseph Hawes and N. Ray Hiner (Westport, Conn.: Greenwood Press, 1985). An older and briefer, but still useful, treatment is Robert R. Sears, *Your Ancients Revisited: A History of Child Development* (Chicago and London: University of Chicago Press, 1975). Another account based on the extensive interviews with pioneers in the field of child development is Milton Senn, *Insights on the Child Development in the United States* (Chicago: University of Chicago Press, 1975). Transcripts of the interviews conducted by Senn are available through the National Library of Medicine. Important manuscript collections include the Arnold Gesell papers at the Library of Congress, the Lawrence Frank papers at the National Library of Medicine, the Icie Macy Hoobler papers at the Bentley Historical Library, and the very rich collections of the papers of psychologists in the History of Psychology Archives at the University of Akron, including the papers of Jean Macfarlane, Lois B. Murphy, and Mary Cover Jones. Publications from the growth studies done through the University of California–Berkeley were scarce, but a useful compilation is Mary Cover Jones, Nancy Bayley, Jean Walker Macfarlane, and Marjorie Pyles Honzik, eds., *The Course of Human Development: Selected Papers from the Longitudinal Studies, Institute of Human Development, The University of California, Berkeley* (Waltham, Mass.: Xerox College Publishing, 1971).

Tracing the interface between science and culture as this affected young men is Joseph Kett's *Rites of Passage: Adolescence in America, 1790 to the Present* (New York: Basic Books, 1977), and showing the extreme gender bias of early psychology in the United States is Rosalind Rosenberg, *Beyond Separate Spheres: The Intellectual Roots of Modern Feminism* (New Haven: Yale University Press, 1982). For a clear introduction to American social sciences (especially anthropology), see Margaret M. Caffrey, *Ruth Benedict: Stranger in This Land* (Austin: University of Texas Press, 1989). Another broad account of the early twentieth century is Dorothy Ross, *The Origins of American Social Science* (New York: Cambridge University Press, 1991). The best treatment of the child guidance movement in the 1920s and 1930s is Margo Horn, *Before It's Too Late: The Child Guidance Movement in the United*

States, 1922–1945 (Philadelphia: Temple University Press, 1989). A critical assessment of the implications of the rise of social science and especially "experts" in child care and family matters is Christopher Lasch, *Haven in a Heartless World: The Family Besieged* (New York: Basic Books, 1977).

Social Agencies (Chapter 6)

An outstanding overview of public social agencies devoted to children is Joan Gittens, *Poor Relations: The Children of the State in Illinois, 1818–1990* (Urbana and Chicago: University of Illinois Press, 1994). There is a vast literature on social welfare history in the United States covering the 1920s and 1930s. Among the better recent accounts are Beverly Stadum, *Poor Women and Their Families: Hard Working Charity Cases, 1900–1930* (Albany: State University of New York Press, 1992); Murray Levine and Adeline Levine, *Helping Children: A Social History* (New York: Oxford University Press, 1992); Molly Ladd-Taylor, *Women, Child Welfare, and the State* (Urbana: University of Illinois Press, 1994); Robyn Muncy, *Creating a Female Dominion in American Reform, 1890–1935* (New York: Oxford University Press, 1991); Sonya Michel, "Children's Interests/Mother's Rights: Women, Professionals, and the American Family, 1920–1945" (Ph.D. diss., Brown University, 1986); and two works by Linda Gordon, *Heroes of Their Own Lives: The Politics and History of Family Violence, Boston 1880–1960* (New York: Viking, 1988) and *Pitied but Not Entitled: Single Mothers in the History of Welfare, 1890–1935* (New York: Free Press, 1994). An older but useful work is Emma O. Lundberg, *Unto the Least of These: Social Services for Children* (New York: Appleton Century Crofts, 1947). For the special circumstances of African-Americans see Cheryl Greenberg, *Or Does It Explode? Black Harlem in the Great Depression* (New York: Oxford University Press, 1991) and Andrew Billingsley and Jeanne Giovannoni, *Children of the Storm: Black Children and American Child Welfare* (New York: Harcourt, Brace and Jovanovich, 1972). A number of useful manuscript collections of social agencies can be found at the Western Reserve Historical Society in Cleveland, Ohio, including the Cleveland Children's Aid Society, the Family Service Association, and the Youth Service Association. An especially rich set of papers is the records of the Detroit YMCA at the Bentley Historical Library in Ann Arbor, Michigan.

The development of child guidance clinics and their evolution into clinics for problem children is traced in Margo Horn, "Inventing the Problem Child: 'At Risk' Children in the Child Guidance Movement of the 1920s and 1930s," in *Children at Risk in America: History, Concepts, and Public Policy,* ed. Roberta Wollons (Albany: State University of New York Press, 1993), 141–53; and in Margo Horn, *Before It's Too Late: The Child Guidance Movement in the United States, 1922–1945* (Philadelphia: Temple University Press, 1989). See also George S. Stevenson, "Child Guidance and the National

Committee for Mental Hygiene," in *Orthopsychiatry 1923–1948: Retrospect and Prospect,* ed. Lawson G. Lowery and Victoria Sloan (New York: American Orthopsychiatric Association, 1948). For the depression and its impact on social agencies see Robert S. McElvaine, *The Great Depression: America, 1929–1941* (1984; reprint, New York: Times Books, 1993). J. Stanley Lemons, "The Sheppard-Towner Act: Progressivism in the 1920s," *Journal of American History* 65 (1969): 776–86, treats Sheppard-Towner adequately, but see also Kristie Lindenmeyer, *"A Right to Childhood": The U.S. Children's Bureau and Child Welfare, 1912–1946* (Urbana: University of Illinois Press, forthcoming). Two important dissertations have also looked at the Children's Bureau and the administration of Sheppard-Towner: Nancy Pottishman Weiss, "Save the Children: A History of the Children's Bureau, 1903–1918," (Ph.D. diss., University of California–Los Angeles, 1974) and Louis J. Covotsos, "Child Welfare and Social Progress: A History of the United States Children's Bureau, 1912–1935" (Ph.D. diss., University of Chicago, 1976). An older institutional history of the bureau is Dorothy E. Bradbury, *Five Decades of Action for Children: A History of the Children's Bureau* (Washington, D.C.: Social Security Administration, Children's Bureau, 1962). See also Charles King, *Children's Health in America: A History* (New York: Twayne, 1993).

Children in the Depression and the New Deal (Chapter 7)

The most important work regarding the impact of the depression on children's lives is Glen Elder, *Children of the Great Depression: Social Change in Life Experience* (Chicago: University of Chicago Press, 1974). The literature on the great depression is voluminous. A useful overview is Robert S. McElvaine, *The Great Depression: America, 1929–1941* (New York: Times Books, 1993 [c 1984]), but best at capturing the way people felt and coped is Studs Terkel, *Hard Times: An Oral History of the Great Depression* (New York: Washington Square Press, 1970). In that same category, see Robert J. Hastings, *A Nickel's Worth of Skim Milk: A Boy's View of the Great Depression* (Carbondale, Ill.: Southern Illinois University Press, 1972). William E. Leuchtenburg, *Franklin Roosevelt and the New Deal, 1932–1940* (New York: Harper and Row, 1963) remains a standard overview. A recent and provocative work, Colin Gordon, *New Deals: Business, Labor, and Politics in America, 1920–1935* (New York: Cambridge University Press, 1994), 161–67, offers some new interpretations. See also Irving Bernstein, *A Caring Society: The New Deal, the Worker, and the Great Depression* (Boston: Houghton Mifflin, 1985), which looks at the circumstances of working-class Americans, and Terry A. Cooney, *Balancing Acts: American Thought and Culture in the 1930s* (New York: Twayne Publishers, 1995). A useful guide to the literature pertaining to children and youth in the period is Leroy Ashby, "The Depression and World War II," in *American Childhood, A Research Guide and Historical Handbook,* ed. Joseph M. Hawes and N. Ray Hiner (Westport, Conn.:

Greenwood Press, 1985). An outstanding collection for tracing the impact of the depression on children's lives is the records of the Children's Fund of Michigan in the Bentley Historical Library in Ann Arbor, Michigan. Also in that repository are the papers of Arthur Dunham and Michael Church, both longtime social welfare administrators.

The follow-up to their famous study of the 1920s in a medium-sized American city (Muncie, Indiana), Robert S. Lynd and Helen Merrill Lynd's *Middletown in Transition: A Study in Cultural Conflicts* (New York: Harcourt Brace, 1937) shows how much of society was affected by the depression. Other works dealing with some of the effects of the depression include Charles King, *Children's Health in America: A History* (New York: Twayne, 1993); Joseph M. Hawes, *The Children's Rights Movement: A History of Advocacy and Protection* (Boston: Twayne, 1991); Walter Trattner, *From Poor Law to Welfare State: A History of Social Welfare in America* (New York: Free Press, 1974); and Winifred Bell, *Aid to Dependent Children* (New York: Columbia University Press, 1965). The story of the National Youth Administration is told in Betty Lindley and Ernest K. Lindley, *A New Deal for Youth: The Story of the National Youth Administration* (New York: Viking Press, 1938) and more recently in Richard Reiman, *The New Deal and American Youth: Ideas and Ideals in a Depression Decade* (Athens: University of Georgia Press, 1992). Margaret O'Brien Steinfels's *Who's Minding the Children? The History and Politics of Day Care in America* (New York: Simon and Schuster, 1973) traces the history of publicly funded day care, including the WPA nursery schools. The origins and development of Social Security can be followed in Edwin E. Witte, *The Development of Social Security* (Madison: University of Wisconsin Press, 1962) and Roy Lubove, *The Struggle for Social Security, 1900–1935* (Cambridge: Harvard University Press, 1968). The final report of the 1940 White House Conference on Children and Youth is Conference on Children and Youth in a Democracy, *Final Report* (Washington, D.C.: Government Printing Office, 1940).

Index

The Author

Joseph M. Hawes is a professor of history at the University of Memphis. His most recent book is *The Children's Rights Movement: A History of Advocacy and Protection* (Twayne, 1991).

The Editor

N. Ray Hiner is Chancellors' Club Teaching Professor of History and Education at the University of Kansas. He has published widely on the history of children and education in the United States and is coeditor (with Joseph M. Hawes) of *Growing Up in America* (1985), *American Childhood* (1985), *Children in Historical Perspective* (1991), and Twayne's History of American Childhood Series. He is writing a book about children in the life and thought of Cotton Mather.